MW01148784

Driving Career Results

How to Manage Self-Directed Employee Development

Linda Brenner

Publisher: Paul Boger
Editor-in-Chief: Amy Neidlinger
Acquisitions Editor: Charlotte Maiorana
Cover Designer: Alan Clements
Managing Editor: Kristy Hart
Project Editor: Lori Lyons
Copy Editor: Apostrophe Editing Services
Proofreader: Paula Lowell
Indexer: Erika Millen
Compositor: Nonie Ratcliff
Manufacturing Buyer: Dan Uhrig

Old Tappan, New Jersey 07675

For information about buying this title in bulk quantities, or for special sales opportunities (which may include electronic versions; custom cover designs; and content particular to your business, training goals, marketing focus, or branding interests), please contact our corporate sales department at corpsales@pearsoned.com or (800) 382-3419.

For government sales inquiries, please contact governmentsales@pearsoned.com.

For questions about sales outside the U.S., please contact international@pearsoned.com.

Company and product names mentioned herein are the trademarks or registered trademarks of their respective owners.

Printed in the United States of America

First Printing December 2015

ISBN-10: 0-13-438164-5
ISBN-13: 978-0-13-438164-0

Pearson Education LTD.
Pearson Education Australia PTY, Limited
Pearson Education Singapore, Pte. Ltd.
Pearson Education Asia, Ltd.
Pearson Education Canada, Ltd.
Pearson Educación de Mexico, S.A. de C.V.
Pearson Education—Japan
Pearson Education Malaysia, Pte. Ltd.

Library of Congress Control Number: 2015954137

Contents at a Glance

Contents

Acknowledgments

To the many people who inspired and influenced this work, including Kerri, Sharon, Holly, Lauran, Rebecca, Cecilia, Lauren, Mandy, Jaime, Scott, and Andy.

And to those who've made it possible for me to love what I do, including Gregg, Josh, Max, Lynne, and my Mom and Dad.

About the Author

Linda Brenner started Designs on Talent (www.designsontalent.com) in 2004 with the vision of helping business leaders improve talent results. She then founded Skillsify, Inc. (www.skillsify.com) in 2012 as a way to scale and improve hiring and retention results. The firms' clients include great brands such as Coca-Cola, IHG, Amazon, Expedia, AT&T, Chick-fil-A, L'Oreal, Ogilvy, and Turner Broadcasting. Linda is also the coauthor of *Talent Valuation: Accelerate Market Capitalization through Your Most Important Asset* (Pearson, 2015, available on Amazon.com).

Linda's innovative, results-oriented approach is coupled with a bias for action and a focus on measurable results. This same orientation is reflected throughout her team of talent acquisition, talent management, and finance experts.

Prior to founding Designs on Talent, Linda spent her professional career leading talent acquisition and talent management teams for Gap, Pepsi/Pizza Hut, and Home Depot. Linda had a variety of roles at The Home Depot before leading the company's retail talent acquisition function. In addition to centralizing TA for the first time in the company's history, under Linda's leadership, Home Depot became the largest government contractor in the United States and forged first-of-their-kind partnerships with AARP, the Department of Defense, and the Department of Labor.

Linda holds a Master of Arts degree in Labor and Employment Relations and a Bachelor of Arts degree in Judaic Studies, both from University of Cincinnati. She and her family live in Atlanta.

You can reach Linda at: linda@skillsify.com.

1

The Importance of Driving
Your Own Development

Not long ago, most employees could sit back and wait for their manager to "develop" them. The burden was on the shoulders of the leaders to identify the employee's needs, create a plan for how to address those needs, and then provide the employee with ongoing feedback and coaching.

Those days are long gone. Managers these days are rarely expected to, or held accountable for, developing their people. In reality, it never worked well. Managers often didn't have the tools, expertise, or information to do a good job developing their employees. Over time, it seems that organizations have simply given up. And it's easy to see why. In the last 20 years, it's become nearly impossible to expect such work from managers. After all, their span of control has grown to the point in which it's unwieldy to do much more than share basic communication with their employees. In addition, changes in the workplace have reduced the opportunity for managers to observe their employees and provide timely, in-the-moment feedback. The advent of the virtual workplace, global teams, and nontraditional workers, such as contract employees, have added even more challenges to the old model. Lastly, managers still often lack the resources and knowledge to develop their employees in a targeted, meaningful, and successful way.

Even the expectation that managers will write annual performance reviews is waning. According to a 2015 PwC survey, an estimated 5% of organizations in 2015 are projected to join companies such as Accenture, Adobe, Microsoft, and Netflix in dropping their traditional, manager-led performance review approach.

If managers aren't expected to complete annual performance reviews, what hope is there that they'll create development plans for their people?

Very little.

Employees—and job seekers—must be in charge of their own learning and development and, ultimately, their career path. In truth, not just "employees" but any type of worker, including contractors, consultants, seasonals, temporary, part-time, virtual, interns, and such. Bottom line: We all own our own development.

As mentioned, managers often lack the information, resources, and know-how to drive their employees' development. So if we take them out of the equation, what are employees left with? How can they drive their own learning, development, and improvement?

The purpose of this book is to put information into the hands of employees—and job seekers—so that they can be in the driver's seat of their own career development. In that sense, consider this book a roadmap to help you drive between points along your career path.

This book is also written for HR leaders who seek to change the old, outdated, and nearly impossible model of manager-led development planning.

Whether you're an employee seeking to advance your career, a job seeker, or an HR leader, this book is for you. It provides you with a step-by-step guide for taking control and achieving your personal career goals.

Frequently Asked Questions About Self-Directed Development

What is a development plan?

A *development plan* is a documented, personalized plan for guiding an individual's career aspirations. It identifies the person's strengths, along with goals for leveraging them, and areas for improvement, with plans for practicing and improving (see Figure 1.1). Development plans include manager input, concrete goals, timelines, roles, and desired outcomes. Inputs to development plans include feedback from performance reviews, assessments, informal feedback, input from clients, and performance-related data.

What It Is	What It Is NOT
• An on-going process	• A one-time event
• Owned by the team member and supported by the manager	• Owned by the manager
• Focused on specific areas of strengths and needs	• Nebulous, vague, not specific – or focused only on weaknesses
• Includes goals and commitments	• Doesn't include specific commitments
• Balances team member's needs and the needs of the business	• Is more focused on team member's needs than the business – or vice versa
	• A path to – or guarantee for – promotion

Figure 1.1 What do we mean by "development planning"?

Who creates a development plan?

Traditionally, managers were responsible for building a development plan for their employees. Today, it's the employee's responsibility to create their own plan with input from their manager and other key leaders or co-workers. When employees create their own plan and take action to achieve goals within that plan, they can begin driving their own learning, development, and career management, rather than waiting for others to do it for them. In the end, no one cares about our career more than we do—so it's up to us to get in the driver's seat and get ourselves to the next destination.

What if I don't have a job and can't get input from a manager?

In such a case, you should identify friends, relatives, former co-workers, or classmates—people whom you trust and consider their input valuable—to provide insights, guidance, and feedback. This can be just as valuable as information provided in a work setting, particularly because our individual strengths and needs carry over in all aspects of our lives. In addition, sometimes our friends and family members—over co-workers—are more committed to helping us improve and will be more honest with their feedback!

What is the goal of a development plan?

The goal is to help an individual be more successful in the workplace. This is typically accomplished by identifying a person's strengths and identifying concrete, time-bound ways that he can leverage those strengths, as well as areas of opportunities and specific ways to practice and improve on them. Ultimately, a plan should help an individual work more effectively with others and achieve work-related goals in a more efficient and effective way. As the workplace and our economy changes, our ability to adapt, learn on-the-fly, give and receive feedback, and demonstrate an interest in helping out in different parts of the business will be key to long-term success in any role or with any company.

What is included in a development plan?

The strengths to leverage and areas to improve that are at the core of a person's development plan should come from feedback over time from others. This feedback could be in the form of performance reviews, work results, client or customer feedback, 360° survey feedback, or even input from friends, trusted advisors, or a spouse. The topics included in a development plan should focus on key themes related to a person's strengths and needs. For example, David consistently misses deadlines and has for years. This is a problem that has affected him at school and then later at work. "Missing deadlines" should be reflected in his development plan as an area he should improve. David should talk to his manager and perhaps a trusted peer to determine why he misses deadlines. Is it an inability to prioritize, manage time, estimate how much time tasks will take, make decisions, and so on?

If I write my own plan, what is then the role of my manager in development planning?

An employee's manager is critical (and always has been) to the employee's success on the job. A manager should be viewed as a coach, and an employee should seek out her feedback regarding strengths, needs, ideas for improving, and career aspirations and opportunities. Managers should review key elements of a development plan, specific goals, learnings and outcomes, as well as provide feedback to the employee on a regular basis. Employees can help ensure this happens by scheduling regular time on a manager's calendar to review progress, activities, learnings, and outcomes. Also, seeking a manager's input on developmental goals and career objectives should be a key priority for employees in this process.

What if there is no money available for training classes or resources to help me develop?

This book proves to you that, often, the best development you can receive is free. Working with trusted peers, influential leaders, skilled co-workers, or smart friends to complete specific tasks that help you practice and improve costs nothing. Completing online courses, reading academic articles or blogs, and watching videos such as "Ted Talks" or free training videos from reputable sources can all be excellent ways to learn and improve skills.

How often should a development plan be written?

It used to be a common (and poor) practice that a development plan was written once a year and then, at the time of the performance appraisal, was reviewed by the manager and the employee. This, however, is an ineffective practice. In reality, most people need to work on certain behaviors that must be practiced and improved over time. For example, Nicole works in Operations and often has to collaborate with her peers in Finance, Human Resources, and Marketing. However, she struggles to influence these peers, which hampers her ability to get work completed in a timely way. For Nicole to improve her influencing skills, she will have to practice and improve over time—perhaps for years—in areas such as verbal and nonverbal communication, listening, and identifying mutually beneficial goals. This isn't something she can improve by simply taking a class or practicing once or twice.

What's the best way to improve in a particular area?

The concept of "70-20-10" is a long-standing belief that the way people learn new skills is by 70% doing (or on-the-job training), 20% from other people, and 10% from formal classroom-based or book learning (see Figure 1.2). Others have characterized 70-20-10 as experiential, social, and formal. In any event, hands-on training is a great way for adults to learn, but sometimes it's not easy to figure out practical, hands-on activities that can help us learn. Therefore, this book is chock-full of such ideas for leveraging strengths and improving opportunity areas. Ultimately, practice and feedback and then more practice, repetitively, can drive improvement.

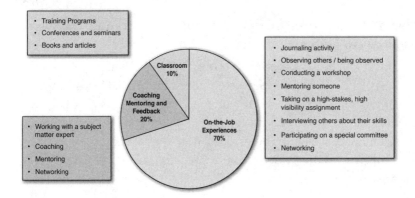

Figure 1.2 A successfully proven approach: 70-20-10

How should development plans be evaluated?

A plan of any kind should contain measurable goals. Most often in a development plan, goals are time-bound. For example, Flora was working to improve her interviewing skills. One of her goals included observing an interview conducted by a peer considered to be an excellent interviewer and debriefing how he prepared for and conducted the interview. Flora committed to completing this within 60 days and discussing her learnings with her manager. In this case, it's easy to determine whether Flora completed her goal in a timely way. Other measures can be used, too. For instance, Flora could track how many candidates that she recommended for hire were actually hired, and then, of those, how many performed well on the job.

Can anyone help me with my development plan?

Certainly. Collaborating with others is a great way to drive learning and development. Consider those within your organization (or your circle of friends and acquaintances) who can help you learn and develop (see Figure 1.3). Use them for advice and to give you feedback, review your work, observe you give a presentation, and more. Of course, it's recommended that you collaborate with people who are skilled in areas that are important to your career growth. This book contains many ways that you can collaborate with others during the course of your development.

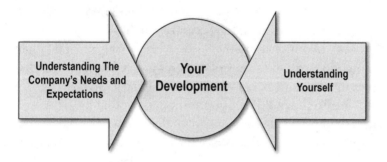

Figure 1.3 What are the key influences on development?

Should I try to improve my "functional" skills or "soft" skills?

Sometimes, individuals need to improve functional skills to be more successful in a particular role or to achieve a wanted promotion. In this case, *functional skills* refers to essential skills that are critical to completing the technical aspect of a job. For example, this might mean programming for someone working in IT, market research for someone working in Marketing, change management for a person working in Human Resources, and so on. It could also refer to a specific software program such as Microsoft Excel. In any case, learning a functional skill might be the focus of a development plan. However, more often, individuals struggle in a role, not because of their lack of a functional skill set, but because of soft skills that they lack or struggle to master. *Soft skills* are personality traits associated with communication, collaboration, leading people, reading situations, managing emotions, and such. An inability to demonstrate these skills is the most common reason why people struggle in roles—particularly as they are promoted to positions with greater responsibilities. For this reason, development plans often focus on soft skills. These are also the types of skills that can take a long time (in some cases years) for individuals to master or even simply improve.

If I complete a development plan, will I get promoted?

Although there isn't a clear or guaranteed link between taking action on a personal development plan and receiving a promotion, the two are closely related. Let's first talk about why these two issues, development and promotions, are not linked. First, most companies have more people who want to be promoted than opportunities for promotions. As you move up in the organization, fewer roles exist and there is more competition for them. Second, just because an individual seeks a promotion, or a different role of any kind, it doesn't mean that he deserves it, is the best person for it, or is the most qualified person to be appointed to the position. Simply wanting another job, and even taking steps to improve, doesn't guarantee that the move will happen. However, often employees don't have the chance to leverage all their strengths on the job and therefore fail to demonstrate critical reasons why they should be considered for other opportunities. However, we all have areas that we can improve, and sometimes these get in the way of succeeding in our current roles.

The intent of this book is to help employees improve their performance in their current role so that they can demonstrate their readiness for the next level role or additional responsibility (see Figure 1.4). It is also a resource for those who are seeking a job, such as a college student or an individual out of work, by helping them leverage their strengths and improve their areas of needs in a variety of nonwork settings.

What's the difference between a development plan and a performance review?

The focus of a development plan should be behaviors related to our strengths and needs, which may not change often. A performance review relates to specific goals relative to a particular job. For instance, if Anika needs to improve her delegating skills, she will likely be working on that over time, regardless of her specific role. However, her performance review goals will change regularly, perhaps annually and certainly if she were to change jobs.

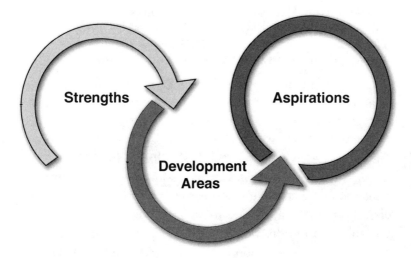

Figure 1.4 Understanding yourself

If a development plan doesn't result in a promotion, then what's the point?

The point is, in order to succeed, we must adapt. Adaptation comes from learning, evolving, growing, and changing our behaviors. The purpose of this book is to help you take control of what you learn and how you learn it, instead of putting your career destiny entirely into the hands of others. Although learning and improving may not result in an immediate and concrete result (you are awarded with a promotion, for example), it provides you with opportunities to interact with others, try new approaches, have meaningful discussions with people from whom you can learn, and challenge yourself to adapt and grow.

What's the role of my HR partner in my development?

You should consider your HR partner a key stakeholder in your development. Your HR partner can be a source of feedback, development suggestions, training resources, learning tools, and connections to mentors and informal coaches. She can also help guide you regarding what you should be working on, how to learn about other roles within the organization, and how to navigate different situations and personalities. Like many in your circle of personal and professional acquaintances, your HR partner can help you build a learning and development plan as well as work toward your career goals.

What's the best way to build an Individual Development Plan?

Your company may have a template for an Individual Development Plan (IDP) or access to a technology that powers development planning. For instance, enterprise-wide human capital technology systems such as Workday, Oracle, and Taleo have "Development Planning" modules containing web-based forms for building your plan. Often, organizations have Learning Management Systems with e-learning modules and other resources for training and development planning. If you don't have access to such tools or technology, you can find a template within this book (and in Chapter 8, specifically) that you can reference. In addition, you can search online for development plan templates and find a variety in different formats, such as MS Word or Excel.

How will I know that I've improved?

It depends on what kinds of skills you want to improve. For example, if you want to learn a software package, such as Access or Excel, it is relatively easy to determine if you've mastered the aspects of the program. You can even complete an online skills assessment to objectively assess, and perhaps share with your manager, the outcomes of your efforts and learning. However, if you're working on a soft skill such as business writing, you will need to get others to comment on the extent to which you've improved. If you're working on a behavior such as decision making or prioritization, a great way to assess the degree to which you've learned and improved is through the use of an assessment tool such as 360° Feedback. With 360° Feedback, others complete anonymous surveys about your behavior. It's called "360°" because feedback is typically gathered from a variety of sources, including direct reports, peers, senior leaders, and others. When completed at different points over time, it provides a more quantitative way to track progress from how others observe you. If a 360° Feedback program isn't available to you, relying on simply asking others for their feedback on how you're improving can be effective.

If I'm a people leader, what can I do to encourage my employees to develop their own plan?

Share this book with them! Talk to them about the importance of driving their own development and of the value of determining what strengths they most need to leverage and what areas they most need to develop (see Figure 1.5). Ask them to share their thoughts with you and talk about how they identified these developmental goals. Talk to them about how to build a plan and give them concrete action steps. Review their plan with them and help to ensure it's realistic and meaningful. Ask them to set up 15-minute meetings monthly to review their progress, actions, and outcomes. Last, provide regular feedback about how they're performing and improving. Along the way, recognize progress and great performance. Share successes and encourage the leveraging of strengths among the team.

Development Planning. . .

- We can ALL improve
- Our business demands that we continuously learn, develop, collaborate and improve
- We each need a unique way to plan our own learning and development:
    - What strengths we most need to leverage
    - What areas we most need to improve
    - How we want to work it
    - When we want to work it
    - With whom we want to collaborate

Figure 1.5 Reasons development planning is critical

How This Book Is Organized

This book is intended for use by anyone who seeks to improve their skills in the workplace. It can help you identify—through a self-assessment as well as self-reflection questions about feedback you've received in the past—your greatest strengths and needs. It can then act as a resource guide to enable you to quickly zero in on specific ways you can leverage your strengths and ideas for driving specific areas of improvement. It presents dozens of practical, bite-sized, free development suggestions for you to consider and add to a development plan. The suggestions in this book should not be seen as an all-inclusive list; they should inspire you to create your own development activities that reflect your work (or school), interests, and learning preferences.

Here's how we recommend you proceed. Thanks for taking time to invest in yourself!

1. Complete your self-assessment.
2. Consider other feedback you've received in the past.
3. Identify one or two greatest strengths.
4. Use the resource guide to identify specific ways to leverage your strengths.
5. Identify one or two greatest opportunities for improvement.
6. Use the resource guide to identify specific ways to improve your areas of opportunity.
7. Build a plan by documenting these action steps, add dates for completion, and if appropriate, others with whom you can collaborate.
8. If appropriate, review your plan with your manager.
9. Set up regular, quick updates with your manager or a trusted advisor on the calendar to review your plan, activities completed, lessons learned, and progress made.
10. Continue to work your plan by noting which activities you've completed, adding more, expanding into other areas of strength and need, and collaborating with others over time.

Assess Yourself

Creating a development plan can be a daunting task—especially when you're searching for a new job or seeking to drive your career forward. Sometimes, it's hard to identify what, specifically, you need to improve to be more successful. And even after you identify a specific area, it's not obvious what to do to practice and improve at it. In addition, you might be overly focused on opportunity areas and forget all the strengths you have and how to leverage them more effectively.

This book solves these two critical challenges:

1. Identify the most important areas to improve and your greatest strengths to leverage.
2. Create hundreds of development suggestions that are practical, bite-sized, self-directed, and free.

Before You Begin

To identify your strengths and needs, you can use a simple self-survey that enables you to assess your skills in just a few minutes (see Figure 1.6). This survey is based on competencies and behaviors that are universally important for career success. The only rule you need to follow to get the most out of the survey is to be completely honest with yourself. After all, no one will see this but you unless you decide to share your results with someone else. Remember, you are in the driver's seat of your career, so tell the truth and see where this road takes you.

When completing the survey, consider your answer as it relates to your current or most recent job. If you're a student, evaluate your response as it relates to collaborating with others on a project or task, or working with your family, in your community, or your place of worship. For example, consider "customers" as people in your life to whom you have responsibilities.

Check the box that best describes you, and when complete, tally your scores in space provided. At the end of the assessment, there are instructions on how to interpret your scores.

If you prefer to do this online, you can contact us (info@skillsify. com) and receive a 30-day license to the SkillBuilder app. You can then complete this assessment online, have your score automatically calculated, and create and manage your development plan within the tool. You can also track your progress over time, collaborate with others virtually, and access your development plan from any location. Developing takes dedication and the tracking of your progress, learnings, and achievements over time. Make it easier and sign up for your free account today.

Let's get started.

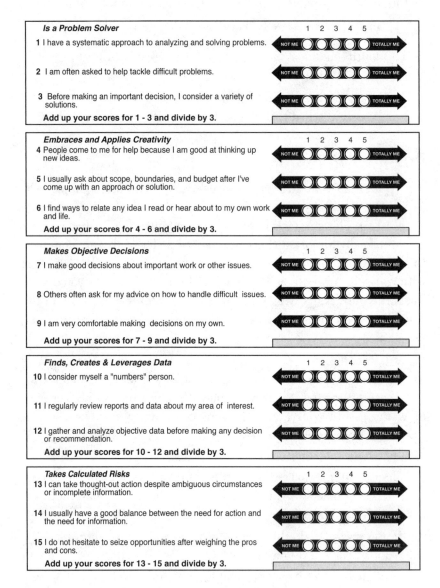

Is a Problem Solver   1 2 3 4 5

1 I have a systematic approach to analyzing and solving problems.   NOT ME ◯◯◯◯◯ TOTALLY ME

2 I am often asked to help tackle difficult problems.   NOT ME ◯◯◯◯◯ TOTALLY ME

3 Before making an important decision, I consider a variety of solutions.   NOT ME ◯◯◯◯◯ TOTALLY ME
Add up your scores for 1 - 3 and divide by 3.

Embraces and Applies Creativity   1 2 3 4 5
4 People come to me for help because I am good at thinking up new ideas.   NOT ME ◯◯◯◯◯ TOTALLY ME

5 I usually ask about scope, boundaries, and budget after I've come up with an approach or solution.   NOT ME ◯◯◯◯◯ TOTALLY ME

6 I find ways to relate any idea I read or hear about to my own work and life.   NOT ME ◯◯◯◯◯ TOTALLY ME
Add up your scores for 4 - 6 and divide by 3.

Makes Objective Decisions   1 2 3 4 5
7 I make good decisions about important work or other issues.   NOT ME ◯◯◯◯◯ TOTALLY ME

8 Others often ask for my advice on how to handle difficult issues. NOT ME ◯◯◯◯◯ TOTALLY ME

9 I am very comfortable making decisions on my own.   NOT ME ◯◯◯◯◯ TOTALLY ME
Add up your scores for 7 - 9 and divide by 3.

Finds, Creates & Leverages Data   1 2 3 4 5
10 I consider myself a "numbers" person.   NOT ME ◯◯◯◯◯ TOTALLY ME

11 I regularly review reports and data about my area of interest.   NOT ME ◯◯◯◯◯ TOTALLY ME

12 I gather and analyze objective data before making any decision or recommendation.   NOT ME ◯◯◯◯◯ TOTALLY ME
Add up your scores for 10 - 12 and divide by 3.

Takes Calculated Risks   1 2 3 4 5
13 I can take thought-out action despite ambiguous circumstances or incomplete information.   NOT ME ◯◯◯◯◯ TOTALLY ME

14 I usually have a good balance between the need for action and the need for information.   NOT ME ◯◯◯◯◯ TOTALLY ME

15 I do not hesitate to seize opportunities after weighing the pros and cons.   NOT ME ◯◯◯◯◯ TOTALLY ME
Add up your scores for 13 - 15 and divide by 3.

Figure 1.6 Skills assessment

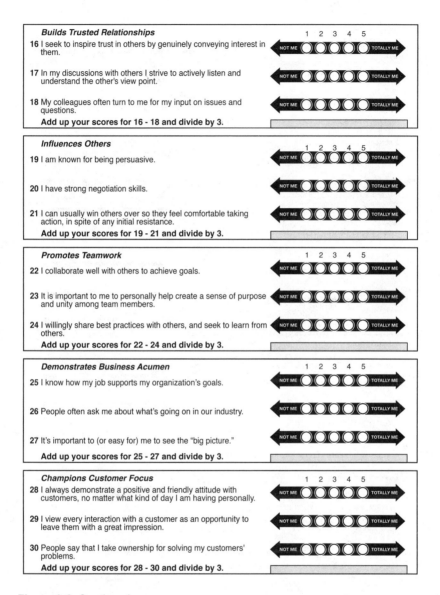

Builds Trusted Relationships

1 2 3 4 5

16 I seek to inspire trust in others by genuinely conveying interest in them.   NOT ME — TOTALLY ME

17 In my discussions with others I strive to actively listen and understand the other's view point.   NOT ME — TOTALLY ME

18 My colleagues often turn to me for my input on issues and questions.   NOT ME — TOTALLY ME

Add up your scores for 16 - 18 and divide by 3.

Influences Others

1 2 3 4 5

19 I am known for being persuasive.   NOT ME — TOTALLY ME

20 I have strong negotiation skills.   NOT ME — TOTALLY ME

21 I can usually win others over so they feel comfortable taking action, in spite of any initial resistance.   NOT ME — TOTALLY ME

Add up your scores for 19 - 21 and divide by 3.

Promotes Teamwork

1 2 3 4 5

22 I collaborate well with others to achieve goals.   NOT ME — TOTALLY ME

23 It is important to me to personally help create a sense of purpose and unity among team members.   NOT ME — TOTALLY ME

24 I willingly share best practices with others, and seek to learn from others.   NOT ME — TOTALLY ME

Add up your scores for 22 - 24 and divide by 3.

Demonstrates Business Acumen

1 2 3 4 5

25 I know how my job supports my organization's goals.   NOT ME — TOTALLY ME

26 People often ask me about what's going on in our industry.   NOT ME — TOTALLY ME

27 It's important to (or easy for) me to see the "big picture."   NOT ME — TOTALLY ME

Add up your scores for 25 - 27 and divide by 3.

Champions Customer Focus

1 2 3 4 5

28 I always demonstrate a positive and friendly attitude with customers, no matter what kind of day I am having personally.   NOT ME — TOTALLY ME

29 I view every interaction with a customer as an opportunity to leave them with a great impression.   NOT ME — TOTALLY ME

30 People say that I take ownership for solving my customers' problems.   NOT ME — TOTALLY ME

Add up your scores for 28 - 30 and divide by 3.

Figure 1.6 Continued

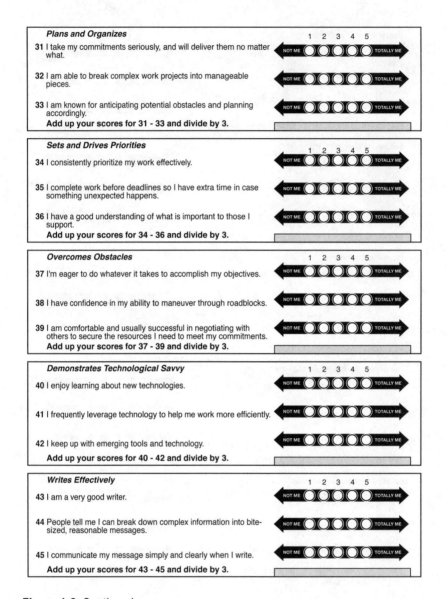

Figure 1.6 Continued

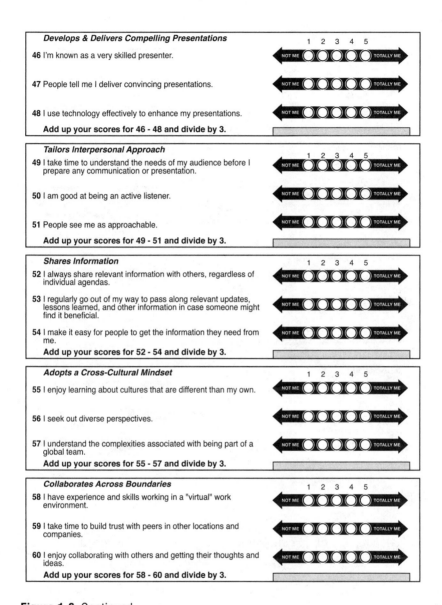

Develops & Delivers Compelling Presentations

46 I'm known as a very skilled presenter.

47 People tell me I deliver convincing presentations.

48 I use technology effectively to enhance my presentations.

Add up your scores for 46 - 48 and divide by 3.

Tailors Interpersonal Approach

49 I take time to understand the needs of my audience before I prepare any communication or presentation.

50 I am good at being an active listener.

51 People see me as approachable.

Add up your scores for 49 - 51 and divide by 3.

Shares Information

52 I always share relevant information with others, regardless of individual agendas.

53 I regularly go out of my way to pass along relevant updates, lessons learned, and other information in case someone might find it beneficial.

54 I make it easy for people to get the information they need from me.

Add up your scores for 52 - 54 and divide by 3.

Adopts a Cross-Cultural Mindset

55 I enjoy learning about cultures that are different than my own.

56 I seek out diverse perspectives.

57 I understand the complexities associated with being part of a global team.

Add up your scores for 55 - 57 and divide by 3.

Collaborates Across Boundaries

58 I have experience and skills working in a "virtual" work environment.

59 I take time to build trust with peers in other locations and companies.

60 I enjoy collaborating with others and getting their thoughts and ideas.

Add up your scores for 58 - 60 and divide by 3.

Figure 1.6 Continued

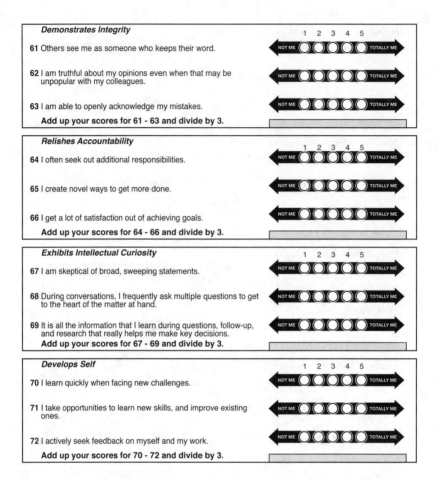

Figure 1.6 Continued

The next set of assessment questions (73–93) are specific to leaders (see Figure 1.7). Skip these if these aren't relevant to you.

Manager Specific

Challenges Norms Appropriately　　1　2　3　4　5

73 I speak up when encountering something that doesn't seem right.　NOT ME ○○○○○ TOTALLY ME

74 I tend to question basic assumptions.　NOT ME ○○○○○ TOTALLY ME

75 I am known for pushing boundaries, but not in an intimidating way.　NOT ME ○○○○○ TOTALLY ME

Add up your scores for 73 - 75 and divide by 3.

Manages Courageously　　1　2　3　4　5

76 I am not afraid to respectfully say what needs to be said.　NOT ME ○○○○○ TOTALLY ME

77 I am known for dealing with problems - people or situation related - fairly and firmly and in a timely manner.　NOT ME ○○○○○ TOTALLY ME

78 I try to be open and forthright when I feel strongly, without appearing threatening.　NOT ME ○○○○○ TOTALLY ME

Add up your scores for 76 - 78 and divide by 3.

Navigates Ambiguity　　1　2　3　4　5

79 I can think and effectively respond to others on the fly.　NOT ME ○○○○○ TOTALLY ME

80 I am known as someone who can shift gears with ease.　NOT ME ○○○○○ TOTALLY ME

81 I am not upset when issues remain unresolved in spite of my best efforts.　NOT ME ○○○○○ TOTALLY ME

Add up your scores for 79 - 81 and divide by 3.

Creates a Culture of Innovation　　1　2　3　4　5

82 I enjoy drawing new ideas and creativity out of my team.　NOT ME ○○○○○ TOTALLY ME

83 I encourage innovative thinking in myself and others.　NOT ME ○○○○○ TOTALLY ME

84 I reflect on learnings from both successes and failures to see what can be improved next time.　NOT ME ○○○○○ TOTALLY ME

Add up your scores for 82 - 84 and divide by 3.

Motivates Others　　1　2　3　4　5

85 People tell me they enjoy working for me.　NOT ME ○○○○○ TOTALLY ME

86 I am known for bringing out the best in the teams I lead.　NOT ME ○○○○○ TOTALLY ME

87 It is important to me that my people feel valued and appreciated.　NOT ME ○○○○○ TOTALLY ME

Add up your scores for 85 - 87 and divide by 3.

Figure 1.7 Manager–specific skills assessment

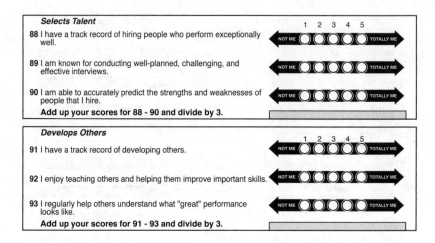

Figure 1.7 Continued

Use the following summary template to enter the scores you calculated for each behavior.

Behavior	Score
Is a Problem Solver	
Embraces and Applies Creativity	
Makes Objective Decisions	
Finds, Creates, & Leverages Data	
Takes Calculated Risks	
Builds Trusted Relationships	
Influences Others	
Promotes Teamwork	
Demonstrates Business Acumen	
Champions Customer Focus	
Plans and Organizes	
Sets and Drives Priorities	
Overcomes Obstacles	
Demonstrates Technological Savvy	
Writes Effectively	
Develops & Delivers Compelling Presentations	

Behavior	Score
Tailors Interpersonal Approach	
Shares Information	
Adopts a Cross-Cultural Mindset	
Collaborates Across Boundaries	
Demonstrates Integrity	
Relishes Accountability	
Exhibits Intellectual Curiosity	
Develops Self	

Behaviors for Leaders	Score
Challenges Norms Appropriately	
Manages Courageously	
Navigates Ambiguity	
Creates a Culture of Innovation	
Motivates Others	
Selects Talent	
Develops Others	

You've completed the Self Survey! Now identify your top strengths and greatest needs based on your highest and lowest scores. Definitions for each of the behaviors are provided in the next section for your reference.

These results provide a great starting point for you to create your individual development plan. You can start with your highest and lowest scoring categories or pick others that are relevant to you based on performance data, feedback you've received in the past, other assessments you've completed, and so on.

The following chapters provide a host of development suggestions for every behavior. You can take this assessment as many times as you like. Developing is a lifelong process. Take it periodically to see how your strengths and needs change over time.

What are your three highest scored items?

Behavior	Score

What other behaviors resonate as personal strengths for you?

Behavior	Score

What are your three lowest scored items?

Behavior	Score

What other opportunity areas do you believe you need to work on?

Behavior	Score

From these lists, identify 1 to 2 strengths to leverage and 1 to 2 areas to develop. Over time, you can add others to your plan.

Definitions of Behaviors

This section includes definitions for each of the behaviors included in the survey.

Is a Problem Solver

How do you know someone is a problem solver? They clearly identify problems (but not only the problem) and consider solutions, too. They analyze the situation and may gather data by asking questions, reviewing information, and seeking others' opinions. They are action-oriented and may offer up a few possible solutions, along with the pros and cons of each. When handling significant problems, they may use more formal problem-solving methodologies or tools.

Embraces and Applies Creativity

What comes to mind when you think about someone who is creative? Creativity isn't just artistic expression; it's a way of viewing and interacting with the world that can enhance all areas of life. A person who embraces and applies creativity generates relevant, original ideas and solutions, or applies ideas and solutions in new ways. They make connections among previously unrelated notions. They recognize the value of bringing in ideas from the outside and are not afraid to experiment to find solutions.

Makes Objective Decisions

What were the best decisions you've made? What helped you make them? A person who makes objective decisions makes good decisions based upon wisdom, analysis, and personal experience. They can articulate the criteria they used yet can also trust and leverage sound intuition. They can effectively weigh pros and cons and can reach conclusions confidently in a timely manner, even under tight deadlines.

Finds, Creates, and Leverages Data

When and how do you use data? People who are skilled at finding, creating, and leveraging data make a big impact with their work. They seek out relevant data to support decision making and influence others. They share their findings with others, incorporating data into presentations with skill. They can successfully analyze and synthesize different data points to reach conclusions. They often use data in innovative ways, harnessing the facts to ensure their work is relevant and meaningful.

Takes Calculated Risks

When is taking a risk a good idea? How big of a risk is too big? Someone who takes calculated risks takes action despite ambiguous circumstances or incomplete information. They show good judgment in balancing the need for information with the need for action.

Builds Trusted Relationships

Think of a friend or co-worker with whom you enjoy working. What are the qualities of your relationship with that person that make it enjoyable to work together? Someone who builds trusted relationships actively develops, maintains, and invests in relationships that inspire trust and mutual respect. They build enduring win-win partnerships and model exceptional two-way communication skills.

Influences Others

Have you had a goal that required others' participation? What did you do to bring them on board to work with you? People who are skilled at influencing others have the ability to build consensus by persuading others. They gain cooperation from others to accomplish their goals and have credibility among peers and managers. They are adept at negotiating to achieve their desired outcomes.

Promotes Teamwork

Think back to your best experiences working as part of a team in either your personal or professional life. What helped make your best team experience successful? Someone who promotes teamwork collaborates well with others to achieve goals. They actively break down barriers between team members and identify and share best practices with others. They create a sense of unity and purpose among team members.

Demonstrates Business Acumen

What does it mean to have business acumen? Someone with *business acumen* understands and leverages economic, financial, customer, and industry information. They can see the big picture and comprehend the structure, logistics, and flow of the organization. They know how their area and their work supports their organization's overall goals and their customers.

Champions Customer Focus

Being customer-focused can mean a variety of things, depending on how you define the word *customer*. The most obvious use of the term refers to customers to whom we're selling products and services. But if that doesn't apply to you, it could mean something else. For instance, if you work in a support function, such as Finance or Human Resources, it could mean customers within the organization: your "internal" customers. It could mean peers, fellow students, or truly anyone whose needs you are responsible for meeting. After you define your customer, *championing* them means consistently providing high customer service standards. People who do this see every customer interaction as an opportunity to leave a great impression. They actively seek to understand their customers' needs and recognize their own role in serving customers. They do what it takes to ensure and exceed customer expectations. They understand the link between service and business results.

Plans and Organizes

Think of people in your life who you would describe as "extremely organized." What systems do they implement? How do they plan? People who can effectively plan and organize select and align their work to best support their organization's goals. They break down work into separate steps and accurately scope out time and resources for each step. They anticipate and prepare for obstacles and establish organizing systems to increase their work efficiency. They manage many projects and priorities at once and store and arrange information (paper and electronic) in a useful and efficient way.

Sets and Drives Priorities

When you have a lot of tasks, how do you decide where to start? If you don't have time to do all the tasks, how do you know which ones are most important? People who set and drive priorities spend time on what's most important. They align the teams they work with and help them see which work has the greatest effect on the end goals. They collaborate and delegate effectively and follow up to ensure the highest-priority work is completed.

Overcomes Obstacles

Think of people you know who are resilient and resourceful. What tools or approaches do they use? Someone who overcomes obstacles gets the job done despite obstacles in process, people, or business. They can maneuver through challenges with skill and confidence. They have a sense of urgency. They adapt when needed and shift gears comfortably. They are skilled at negotiating with others to secure the resources needed to meet their commitments. They call upon connections as needed to resolve issues.

Demonstrates Technological Savvy

Our world moves faster all the time with the constant development of new technologies. How businesses leverage technology can often determine their level of success. People who demonstrate technological savvy are quick and confident adopters of new technologies. They make it a priority to seek out and learn the latest advancements in technology and tools to drive the business forward.

Writes Effectively

A great writer can write clearly and succinctly across a variety of different communication mediums, such as articles, presentations, emails, and such. Great writers break down complex information into bite-sized, readable messages. They write in an engaging and conversational way, use proper grammar, and demonstrate good email etiquette.

Develops and Delivers Compelling Presentations

Think about the best presentation you have ever seen. What made it successful? People who develop and deliver compelling presentations create coherent and convincing presentations using technology effectively to enhance the experience for the audience. They present with authority, poise, and confidence. They command attention and can manage the group process during the presentation.

Tailors Interpersonal Approach

Different skills are required to interact successfully with many different kinds of people. The ability to tailor our interpersonal approach makes us come across as warm and approachable. People who tailor their approach know when and how to adapt their communication style for different types of people. They listen patiently to understand and are good at reading others' reactions. They show empathy for others' experiences.

Shares Information

Sharing the right information at the right time is crucial to communicating well. People who are skilled at sharing information in a workplace provide information people need to know to do their jobs. They are timely with information and share and leverage what they know to help others. They are careful not to over-communicate.

Adopts a Cross-Cultural Mindset

The diversity of people in our country grows every day, and the ability to work with and learn from others different from ourselves is increasingly important. People who adopt a cross-cultural mindset are role models in seeking and respecting diverse perspectives and contributions. At work, they recognize and address the complexities associated with being part of a global team. They seek to understand cultures and norms that are different than their own.

Collaborates Across Boundaries

In today's work world, it's increasingly common for employees to work across boundaries of culture and location. Working with people in different locations presents opportunities to expand the talent and resources you have available to you and your work. It can also be challenging because it's not easy to observe people, and you might not have easy access to the people you work with. People who collaborate well across boundaries take care to build trust and communicate clearly with peers in other locations.

Demonstrates Integrity

What does it mean to demonstrate integrity? People with integrity can be counted on to do the right thing in any situation. They keep confidences and readily admit mistakes. They are direct and truthful. They make ethical judgments in all cases and have a strong moral compass. In demonstrating these behaviors, they fuel relationships of growing trust and mutual respect.

Relishes Accountability

People who relish accountability willingly take responsibility for their actions. They do not make excuses, and they own their successes and failures. They seek out new and different responsibilities and demonstrate confidence in their ability to deliver on results. They follow through on commitments and hold others accountable as well.

Exhibits Intellectual Curiosity

What would you love to learn more about right now? Have you sought out ways to learn more? People who exhibit intellectual curiosity are relentless and versatile learners. They collect information from a wide range of sources and make connections among previously unrelated notions. They enjoy the challenge of unfamiliar tasks and ask meaningful questions. They are personally committed to continuous learning.

Develops Self

What does it mean to develop yourself? People who develop themselves learn quickly when facing new problems. They are open to criticism and feedback. They gain insights from mistakes and are constantly looking for, and taking, opportunities to learn new skills and improve existing ones.

Challenges Norms Appropriately

Think back to a time when you stood up for something you knew was right, even if those around you did not agree. People who challenge norms appropriately demonstrate the courage and initiative to speak up when encountering something that doesn't seem right or when they have a strong conviction. They ask questions assertively and respectfully, and thoughtfully question both their own and others' assumptions. They develop a solid case for change and present alternative solutions without undermining other leaders. They are able to still "fall in line" and show support if their proposed alternatives are not approved.

Manages Courageously

People who manage courageously are open and forthright without being perceived as threatening. They deal with problems (people-related or other) fairly, firmly, and in a timely manner. They act with the view of what is best for their organization long-term. They don't hold back on anything that needs to be said, and say it respectfully so others can hear it. They aren't afraid to take negative action when necessary and shoulder responsibility for their own and team decisions.

Navigates Ambiguity

Sometimes it's not possible to have the information or clarity you would like to have in order to make a decision. People who navigate ambiguity well can comfortably handle uncertainty. They can move forward without complete information and can shift gears with ease. They aren't upset when issues are unresolved, in spite of everyone's best efforts. They are adaptable to change and help lead others through change.

Creates a Culture of Innovation

How comfortable are you with thinking outside the box? People who create a culture of innovation use insightful, often unorthodox, methods to discover and develop new ideas, products, or processes that are viable to the organization. They demonstrate and encourage creativity within their team. They are able to draw out innovative thinking from those around them. They are an advocate for innovation and consider failure as opportunity to learn.

Motivates Others

You often need the cooperation and support of others to accomplish your goals. Motivating those around you is a critical leadership skill. People who motivate others are persuasive and influential. They leverage positive reinforcement to guide and inspire others, and they are committed to bringing out the best in their team. They lead by example and are able to assert themselves without diminishing other leaders.

Selects Talent

How comfortable are you with selecting talent? People who select talent well are a good judge of talent. They ask relevant and probing questions during interviews. They accurately predict how individuals will perform in different situations, and they assemble diverse, talented teams.

Develops Others

Think back to mentors and teachers who had a profound influence on your growth and development. What approaches did they take and what qualities did they have? People who develop others use a structured and sustainable approach to guiding, coaching, and developing others. They have a track record of developing great talent.

Conclusion

Now that you have assessed your skills, you are on your way to creating a development plan that will accelerate your growth and open opportunities. You know what strengths you can leverage and where you have opportunities for growth. The following chapters offer hundreds of development suggestions that are practical, bite-sized, self-directed, and free. Read through the sections that cover your areas for growth and choose one to two development suggestions to try. Start small to avoid getting overwhelmed, and recognize that growth and change happen over time. Look at the sections that cover your strengths to find ways to help others who struggle in that area. Engage those around you in your journey, and ask for support as you need it.

2

Competency: Demonstrates Thinking and Judgment

Behavior 1: Is a Problem Solver

Behavior 2: Embraces and Applies Creativity

Behavior 3: Makes Objective Decisions

Behavior 4: Finds, Creates, and Leverages Data

Behavior 5: Takes Calculated Risks

Overview of Competency

People who demonstrate thinking and judgment are thoughtful and intelligent in their approach to solving problems that arise. Rather than focusing on the challenges, they are solutions-oriented. They look at problems from different angles, apply creativity, question their assumptions, and proactively seek out opposing points of view or evidence to the contrary. Taking a positive outlook, they look for the potential in situations and can move forward without having the total picture.

Behavior 1: Is a Problem Solver

How do you know someone is a problem solver? They clearly identify problems (but not only the problem) and consider solutions, too. They analyze the situation and may gather data by asking questions, reviewing information, and seeking others' opinions. They are action-oriented and may offer a few possible solutions, along with the pros and cons of each. When handling significant problems, they may use more formal problem-solving methodologies or tools.

Ideas for improving this skill:

- **Be more diligent about defining the scope of the problem before finding a solution.** When you're faced with a challenge, make sure you accurately identify the problem and assess options before making a decision. Take time to think through the following:
    - Identify and define the issue. Try to get to the root cause of the problem or opportunity.
    - Look at the issue in different ways. Brainstorm with others to gain different perspectives of the problem.
    - Identify your assumptions. Ask others to help you test whether your assumptions are valid.
    - Ask "who, what, when, where, why, and how": Who is involved? What is occurring? Where is it taking place? When did it occur? Why is it happening? How is it affecting people?

    For the next 30 days, commit to performing this analysis before you make any major decisions. Take time to generate several solutions before deciding upon one. Consider the pros and cons of each. Track how your analysis helps you solve problems.

- **Adopt formal methods and processes for solving problems and making decisions.** Over the next 30-60 days, review the following to help flesh out potential scenarios and hone critical thinking:
    - Decision trees
    - Grid Analysis
    - Fishbone diagramming
    - Cost benefit analysis
    - SWOT Analysis
    - Six Thinking Hats
    - Probability and Statistical Thinking Analysis

    Choose one or two methods to learn about and experiment with over time. Apply one method to a problem in the next 30 days and then discuss the results with your manager or a mentor. How did using the new approach affect the outcome?

- **Find a subject matter expert to help provide additional guidance when facing a tough problem.** Look for someone who has a lot of experience in the industry or has faced a similar problem in another function. Share the problem and the circumstances, and ask them to weigh in. Ask questions like, Have you ever dealt with anything like this before? How did you approach it? How would you handle this situation if you were in my place? Given my ideas/potential solutions, which is the best and why? Which is the worst and why? Consider the responses and choose one or more ideas/tactics to implement. Keep track of the conversations you have with this person over a period of time and identify two to three different specific approaches you can adopt when solving future problems. Make note of how well this works, discuss your learnings with the subject matter expert, and continue to adjust your approach.

- **Seek diverse perspectives on a difficult problem.** When you encounter a complex and persistent problem, seek input from a diverse group of people (in terms of experiences, backgrounds, styles, and such). Use a grid to track the different perspectives, including a column for "Key Learnings" where you identify something unique that you learned from each perspective. Leverage the grid when developing the solution for the problem. Later, reflect on how the solution would have been different and less effective had you not collected input from a diverse group. Record your findings in a journal during the course of managing this complex problem. Later, identify a trusted peer or your manager to review the work you did and what you learned.

- **Explore your problem/issue by learning about both the people who are currently impacted by the problem and those who will benefit from solving it.** Conduct interviews and perform stakeholder analyses to help you understand the nuances of the problem and the best ways to go about solving it. Ask stakeholders questions like, How does this problem impact you? If you were in charge, how would you solve the problem?

How would solving this problem impact your work positively? Negatively? Use the information you gather to take one step toward a solution in the next 30 days.

- **Gather public solutions to a problem by posting it on a subject matter expert website, blog, or LinkedIn Group chat.** Allow people to build on the discussion and leverage the takeaways and input associated with putting several brains on the issue. Use this approach to identify best practices and learn how others outside your organization might handle a similar situation. Record your insights and put one insight into action in the next 30 days.

- **Determine what slows you down when solving problems.** When you're faced with a problem, what makes you hesitate (or undermines your ability) to solve it? Over the next 30 days, keep track of specific problems that are presented to you. Note the problem, who surfaced the problem, what action you take, and the ultimate outcome. Spend some time assessing in each case what slowed you down or created an obstacle. Consider your environment: Is risk-taking rewarded or discouraged? Do you have the data you need? What personal habits, such as procrastination, being disorganized, or uncertainty about the best approach, impede your ability to solve problems? Review your notes with a trusted peer or your manager. Determine at least one change you can make to improve your problem-solving process.

- **Take on a problem with no clear solution.** Within the next 30 to 60 days, ask trusted friends or co-workers to identify a problem they're handling that has no clear steps or outcome to resolving. Offer to help explore and navigate the issue. Learn whatever you can about the circumstances, facts, and people who are involved. Note where the ambiguity is coming from: Are there conflicting opinions from leaders? Are the roles too loosely defined? Meet with these people over a period of time as you propose different approaches to help resolve the issue. Ask for their feedback, and keep track of what you learn. Identify specific tactics that you can use to solve problems in the future.

- **Learn from your past experiences.** Over a period of 30 days, make note of each problem you are faced with solving. Identify a variety of solutions, seek objective data, get input from others, and track your ultimate solution. Then, note the outcome of your decision. What would you do differently, now that you can evaluate the outcome? What additional information do you wish you had originally? As you assess different decisions you make, keep track of learnings and changes you plan to make to your problem-solving process. Review your learnings with a trusted advisor or your manager and ask for feedback. Discuss how you can leverage this information in the future to solve problems more effectively.

- **Learn from those who are known for being great problem solvers.** Identify someone you interact with who is a strong problem solver. Talk to her about how she first identified the problem and then how she reaches solutions to problems. Ask if she has a certain decision-making process to follow, what kinds of data or information she relies on, and from whom she seeks input. Ask what mistakes she has made and how those impacted her future judgments. Make note of her suggestions and ideas, and commit to trying at least two of them over the next 30 days.

- **Read books that emphasize strategies for how to effectively approach and solve problems.** Our list of favorites includes:
  - *Thinking, Fast and Slow* by Daniel Kahneman
  - *Problem Solving 101: A Simple Book for Smart People* by Ken Watanabe
  - *Think Smarter: Critical Thinking to Improve Problem-Solving and Decision-Making Skills* by Michael Kallet

Dedicate at least 30 minutes a week to reading these resources. For a period of 60 days, make note of the things you learn and new things you would like to try. Review these with your manager, a friend, or a co-worker. Discuss how you can incorporate these learnings into your problem-solving routine.

Ideas for leveraging:

Keep track of the problems you solve and the impact they seem to have on others. Share your activity and learnings with others who struggle in this area.

- **Coach someone who wants to improve his problem-solving skills.** Review your approach to resolving issues, and include real-life examples and situations. Learn about his fears; help him determine his biggest areas of opportunity; and suggest your ideas for improvement. Coach him throughout a problem he is facing and share your thinking and feedback regularly. Identify places where he could have taken a better approach and how you've tackled similar problems in the past. Meet with him throughout the process to review his thoughts and concerns. Keep track of your activities and learnings in this area. Assess how effectively you coach and the outcome of progress made.

- **Host a virtual or live lunch-n-learn to discuss strategies for problem solving.** Prepare a discussion around best practices in solving different types of problems. Identify creative workarounds and solutions for overcoming them; use past examples of successes and failures and encourage others to do the same. Share tips and advice and recommend small action steps to help others practice and improve.

- **Develop a short presentation reviewing your problem-solving strategies.** Include tips, best practices, resources, and real-world examples to showcase your experience and knowledge. Include reviews of different problem-solving methodologies. Host a virtual or in-person training session with people who want to improve in this area. As an alternative, share your presentation online: Shoot a short video and post it on You-Tube, or create a PowerPoint presentation and post it on your blog or on another platform.

- **Build a best-practice guide for problem solving.** Include methods you have used successfully, as well as ideas from others such as peers and colleagues. Put the guide into different formats that can be easily accessed by others: website, blog postings, in a group sharing platform, and more.

Behavior 2: Embraces and Applies Creativity

What comes to mind when you think about someone who is creative? Creativity isn't just artistic expression; it's a way of viewing and interacting with the world that can enhance all areas of life. People who embrace and apply creativity generate relevant, original ideas and solutions or apply ideas and solutions in new ways. They make connections among previously unrelated notions. They recognize the value of bringing in ideas from the outside, and they're not afraid to experiment to find solutions.

Ideas for improving this skill:

- **Try new ways to spark creative thinking and find innovative solutions.** Implement these techniques over the next 30 days to see where they take you. Try brainstorming "perfect world" solutions that are ideal, without constraints, even if they are improbable and impossible. This can help you generate creative solutions and identify root causes. Go to the absurd. When working through a problem, identify all the conditions, absolute worst-case and best-case scenarios of the issue at hand to help see the problem from more angles and generate additional solutions. Consider the solutions you might apply if you did or did not have funding. Or as many people. Or physical proximity to others. Or time. Write your solutions down.

- **Give your brain a workout.** Exercising your brain can increase your creativity. For the next eight weeks, make a concerted effort to do one of these tasks at least twice a week: Read the science or technology section of the newspaper or news website. Read a new-to-you blog that focuses on a subject outside of your usual interests or comfort zone. Solve a tough puzzle. Engage in thoughtful arguments. Talk with intelligent people about a meaty topic. Track your efforts in this area in your plan, and note points that you thought were interesting, what was fun or engaging about the activity, or even how you might apply what you learned. After 60 days, you should have at least 16 tasks on your list. Reflect on what you've learned and applied. Did you share an article with someone? Persuade others to share your point of view? Learn about or apply a new model of thinking? Share your process and learnings with a trusted friend or your manager.

- **Examine your biases and push yourself toward break-through thinking.** Creativity can be impaired by our assumptions, biases, and tendencies (that is, attitudes, "go to" solutions, opinions, prejudices, avoidances, and comfort zone issues). Over the next 30 days, pick a problem from work that you regularly face or one process you participate in that could use some improvement. Take a moment to reflect on all your biases and assumptions about how work should be done or what kind of solution should be generated. Record them, and evaluate their validity. Do the assumptions exist because "it's always been that way"? Do they exist because of funding constraints? Could a case be made for changing some of these assumptions? What would new assumptions mean for the process or the range of possible solutions to your problem? Set your assumptions aside and make a concerted effort to leave them out of the problem-solving process for as long as possible. Keep track over the next 30 days of the instances in which you put this approach into action. Make note of your learnings and the outcomes, and reflect on them with your manager or a mentor.

- **Expand your network to include individuals who offer diversity of thought.** When your personal interactions represent many different viewpoints, your thoughts and assumptions will regularly be challenged, and you will be forced to think creatively. Evaluate your network with a critical eye: How diverse is it? What gaps exist? How many people in your network typically have views different from your own? Push yourself to grow the diversity of your network. Look across industries, socio-economic backgrounds, ages, and cultures to find people who can offer unique insight and new ways of thinking through things. When you meet new people, strike up a conversation to learn about their interests or line of work. Send LinkedIn messages or invitations to connect to interesting people, and talk with them over coffee. As you ask them about themselves, think about how their approaches or ideas could possibly be applied to your work. Reach out to three new people over the next 30 days, and record any insights gleaned.

- **Build a library of great thoughts.** Over the next three months, ask people to send you great work—presentations, whitepapers, videos, or articles. Ask for work that describes interesting thought models or approaches, good graphics that explain a "current state" or new idea or that contains provocative articles, videos, or quotations. The age of the document or the discipline from which the presentation came doesn't matter. Read these articles as they come in, and think about ways they could be adapted to your experience. What can you learn from the ideas or problems presented? Make notes of your discoveries. At the end of the three months, review your library with your manager or a peer, and share the top three things you learned. Offer to share the best resources with them.

- **Identify and leverage highly creative individuals.** Within the next 30-60 days, find someone who is known for being creative (at work or in other areas of life) and ask her to mentor you. Share your work problems, concerns, or issues with this person regularly, and ask her to weigh in. After each conversation, record what you discovered. How does she see the problem differently than you? What questions does she ask? Who else might she recommend you speak with? How does she approach the situation? What are her major considerations or priorities when tackling the issue? Make note of your learnings and the outcomes.

- **Initiate a "new possibilities" discussion group.** Ask a handful of other colleagues to join you once a week to explore new ideas and creative solutions. Share inspired ideas with each other, read books/articles related to your interests and work and share what you are learning, or watch TED talks (www.ted.com) and conduct a post video dialogue session. Explore the most interesting concepts shared and ask how others will apply these ideas to their work. Each week, create new discussion questions and be prepared to introduce new material. Rotate this responsibility and get everyone involved. Put this approach into action over the next 90 days.

- **Use the Internet and social media to gather new approaches and ideas.** Over the next 30 days, pose an idea for discussion with others involved in your field using appropriate websites or chat rooms. Allow people to build on the discussion and leverage the takeaways and input achieved by putting several brains on the issue. Remember to keep proprietary information to yourself and pose questions broadly. Leverage this approach for the next five challenges you face. Reflect on the new ideas you gained and how the information helped you identify new practices and tools. Share your learnings and outcomes with a trusted friend or supervisor.

- **Research industry giants who inspire possibilities.** Over the next 30 days, identify several people from various industries who are known for spearheading new ideas and creating new possibilities for others. Study techniques they used to identify their ideas and how they aligned with others to make their visions a reality. Find and read articles about them or conduct interviews with them. How did they move from an idea to implementation of an idea? Record key techniques you would like to work on in your own work.

- **Explore books related to developing your creative side.** Consider the following:
  - *Creativity, Inc.: Overcoming the Unseen Forces That Stand in the Way of True Inspiration* by Amy Wallace and Edwin Catmull
  - *Steal Like an Artist: 10 Things Nobody Told You About Being Creative* by Austin Kleon
  - *The Creative Habit: Learn It and Use It for Life* by Twyla Tharp and Mark Reiter
  - *Spark: How Creativity Works* by Julie Burstein

  Dedicate at least 30 minutes per week to reading these resources. For a period of 30 days, make note of the things you learn and new things you'd like to try. Review these with your manager or a friend. Discuss how you can incorporate these learnings into your routine.

- **Watch videos (or listen to podcasts) that focus on optimizing and increasing creativity.** TED Talks feature a number of inspiring 20-minute talks on this and many other subjects.

Go to www.ted.com and search for "Your Elusive Creative Genius" by Elizabeth Gilbert or "How to Build Your Creative Confidence" by David Kelley to get started.

Dedicate at least 30 minutes per week to watching and listening to resources on increasing creativity. For a period of 30 days, make note of the things you learn and new things you'd like to try. Share them with your creativity mentor or your manager.

Ideas for leveraging:

- **Coach someone who seeks to develop his creative thinking.** Review your approach to solving problems and thinking through issues. Share with him the top five resources you use (blogs, websites, columnists, video interviews, and more) to spark your own creativity. Coach him through a creative process and share your thinking and feedback regularly. Identify places where he could have been more creative and gathered more information and opinions to inform their results. Meet with him throughout the process to review his thoughts and concerns.

- **Develop a short presentation reviewing your approach to creative thinking.** Include tips, best practices, resources, and real-world examples or cases to showcase your experience and knowledge. Host a virtual or in-person training session with people who want to improve in this area. As an alternative, share your presentation online: shoot a short video, and post it on YouTube, or create a PowerPoint presentation and post it on your own blog.

- **Host a virtual or live lunch-n-learn to discuss creative thinking/problem-solving.** Prepare a discussion around what it means to leverage creativity in the workplace. Discuss common problems that people face when trying to be creative; use past examples of successes and failures and encourage others to do the same. Share tips and advice and recommend small action steps to help others practice and improve.

- **Write a one-page summary of your best tips for unleashing creativity.** Include brainstorming methods, alternative thinking techniques, online creativity resources, and so on.

Share it with others at your workplace or post it on your blog, website, or other group sharing platform.

Behavior 3: Makes Objective Decisions

What were the best decisions you've made? What helped you make them? People who make objective decisions make good decisions based upon wisdom, analysis, and personal experience. They can articulate the criteria they used yet can also trust and leverage sound intuition. They can effectively weigh pros and cons and can reach conclusions confidently in a timely manner, even under tight deadlines.

Ideas for improving this skill:

- **When faced with a decision, make a checklist to help you think it through. Think about—and write down—the answers to questions like these:**
  - What impact will the outcome have on the situation?
  - What is the best-case scenario? Worst-case scenario?
  - What information/data/input would help make a better decision?
  - What values or guiding principles should be considered?

  Try using this question-and-answer approach for the next five significant decisions you have to make. Ask your manager or a trusted adviser to review your thought process and conclusions. Keep track of the outcomes of your decisions, what you learned, and what you would do differently.

- **Create a decision-making template to help you include all relevant data.** Jot down elements to a decision-making guide that you can use again and again. It may include the following:
  - Consider important and critical facts that are known.
  - Consider important information that is missing and how you can obtain it.
  - How do those impacted feel about the problem or issue?
  - Are there related problems that will be affected by this decision?

o What are the long- and short-term consequences to this decision?

Try this approach for the next five significant decisions you have to make. Ask your manager or a friend to review your thought process. Keep track of the outcomes of your decisions, what you learned, and what you would do differently.

- **When making a key decision, ask yourself who, what, where, when, and why.** Take a few minutes to consider—and write down answers to—questions like:

  o Who is involved?

  o What is occurring?

  o Where is it taking place?

  o When did it occur?

  o Why is it happening?

  o How are people affected by it?

  These basic questions can help you frame your response. Try this approach for the next five significant decisions you have to make. Ask a trusted mentor or supervisor to review your thought process. Keep track of the outcomes of your decisions, what you learned, and what you would do differently.

- **Understand and learn how to manage your biases.** Judgment can be impaired by our assumptions, biases, and tendencies (that is, attitudes, go-to solutions, opinions, prejudices, avoidances, and comfort zone issues). When confronted with an issue or situation, take a moment to reflect on all your biases and assumptions. Record them, set them aside, and make a concerted effort to leave them out of the process for as long as possible. Over the next 30 days, keep track of the instances in which you put this approach into action. Make note of your learnings and the outcomes. Later, share your observations with your manager or a mentor.

- **Take time to generate several solutions to problems before deciding upon one.** Ask for others' opinions, hold a brainstorming session, think of alternatives that people in opposite parts of the company would recommend, and ask people who are new to the organization for their perspective.

Purposefully seek out diverse opinions. List all possible solutions and consider the pros and cons of each. Later, consider the outcomes of these sessions and how comfortable you felt generating solutions with others. Make note of what worked and didn't work. What would you do differently next time? Track your efforts over the next 30 days and then share your learnings with your manager or a trusted peer.

- **Analyze your history of decision making, including the percentage of decisions you were unhappy with.** Within the next 30 days, list several recent, and important, decisions you've made on a piece of paper. Next, put these decisions in categories (people, career, technical, political, and such). Do themes emerge? What kinds of decisions do you make effectively? In what types of situations do you hesitate or struggle? Next, consider what steps you could take to improve your decision making in the area(s) within which you struggle. What other kinds of data or input could you consider? Could you benefit from more time? Could you begin working with a thought partner when confronted with similar issues? Identify specific steps you'll commit to taking to improve your decision making and make notes of them. Over the next 30 to 60 days, keep track of your work in this area, and share your learnings with your manager or a mentor.

- **Analyze two major decisions made by two leaders you know.** Within the next 30 days, identify leaders whom you have access to, and choose two of their major decisions to analyze. Review the situation, relevant causes, and outcomes. If possible, talk with someone involved in the situation, decision making, and outcomes. Ask about the decision-making process they used, the data referenced, and the information or input they wish they had had. What, in hindsight, would they have done differently? Make note of specific decision-making approaches that you can incorporate into your own style. Begin to leverage these learnings over a period of time, when you make key decisions. Keep track of the decisions you make, the outcomes, and learnings. Discuss this information with your manager or a trusted advisor.

- **Identify a trusted peer who is known to make good decisions regularly.** Over the next 60 days, ask to observe her decision-making process in action, such as responding to emails and leading a meeting. Later, ask about her decision-making process, the kind of input she considered, mistakes she made in the past, and lessons learned. Ask for her advice and guidance when handling tough issues. Keep track of your work in this area, and share your learnings with your manager or a friend.

- **Adopt formal methods and processes for making decisions and leveraging stronger judgment.** Over the next 30-60 days, review the following to help flesh out potential scenarios and hone critical thinking:
  - Decision trees
  - Grid Analysis
  - Fishbone diagramming
  - Cost benefit analysis
  - SWOT Analysis
  - Six Thinking Hats
  - Probability and Statistical Thinking Analysis

  Choose and learn about one or two to methods to experiment with over the next 30 days. Keep track of how they improve your decision making.

- **Research and experiment with different decision-making models and find which ones work for you.** Consider the following models:
  - The Analytic Hierarchy Process
  - The Decision-Thinking Process
  - The Scientific Method
  - The Decision Making Procedure
  - Thought and Knowledge
  - The Paradox of Choice
  - Decisions, Decisions – The Art of Effective Decision Making
  - Decision Phases

The next time you have to make a highly complex decision, consider applying two or three models to help you. Research any you are not yet familiar with and determine which may apply best to your situation. Ask for input from your manager or a trusted peer who you believe makes good decisions. Keep track of your work in this area over the next 60 days.

- **Regularly conduct a "post mortem" on important decisions and judgment calls.** Afterward, ask others who were involved with or impacted by a decision you made for feedback. What did they think went well? What could have been done differently? For each decision, identify two specific things you would do again and two things you would do differently. Document these conversations, learnings, and conclusions over the next 60 days. Recognize and learn from both victories and failures. Keep track of your work in this area, and share your learnings with your manager or a coach.

- **Explore books that illustrate the fundamental attributes of objective decision making.** Consider the following:
  - *Making Decisions: Expert Solutions to Everyday Challenges* by Harvard Business School Press
  - *Blink: The Power of Thinking Without Thinking* by Malcolm Gladwell
  - *Decisive: How to Make Better Choices in Life and Work* by Chip and Dan Heath

  Dedicate at least 30 minutes a week to reading the resources you choose. For a period of 30 days, make note of the things you learn and new things you would like to try. Review these with your manager or a trusted peer. Discuss how you can incorporate these learnings into your routine.

Ideas for leveraging:

- **Coach someone who needs to improve his decision-making skills.** Review your approach to making decisions, big and small. Share your own methodology for gathering facts and analyzing the pros and cons of different options. Interview him about the last few decisions he made, and identify things he could have done differently to produce better outcomes. Meet with him over a period of several weeks, and track his progress in incorporating new approaches and information to his decision-making process.

- **Develop a short presentation about decision making.** Include tips, best practices, resources, and real-world examples and cases to showcase your experience and knowledge. Topics may include the following:
  ○ Decision-making tools and models
  ○ How to analyze data and facts
  ○ When to get a second opinion
- **Host a virtual or in-person training session with people who want to develop their skills in this area.** As an alternative, share your presentation online: Make a short video and post it on YouTube, or create a PowerPoint presentation and post it on your own blog or on another platform.
- **Offer to be a "decision sounding board" for your team.** Be the person others can rely on to bounce their decisions off of, and play the devil's advocate to show them other options. Role-play with them to allow them to justify their decisions out loud.
- **Conduct one-on-one or small group training sessions about decision making.** Ideas include the following:
  ○ Learning from past decisions
  ○ Taking risks when necessary
  ○ Exploration of different decision-making templates and models

Behavior 4: Finds, Creates, and Leverages Data

When and how do you use data? People who are skilled at finding, creating, and leveraging data make a big impact with their work. They seek out relevant data to support decision making and influence others. They share their findings with others, incorporating data into presentations with skill. They can successfully analyze and synthesize different data points to reach conclusions. They often use data in innovative ways, harnessing the facts to ensure their work is relevant and meaningful.

Ideas for improving this skill:

- **When making a decision, use data to answer who, what, when, where, why, and how.** Ask yourself—and take notes about—the following questions:
  - Who is involved?
  - What is occurring?
  - Where is it taking place?
  - When did it occur?
  - Why is it happening?
  - How are people affected by it?

  Gather objective data that can help you respond to each of these questions. Then, using these questions as a framework, organize your response. Over the next 2 months, keep track of the instances in which you put this approach into action. Make note of your learnings and the outcomes. Later, share this information and your decisions with your manager or a trusted advisor.

- **When presenting information, present data visually rather than just reciting numbers.** It is easier to make sense of visual displays than lists of numbers. For example, pie charts illustrate relative proportions; line graphs show changes over time; and bar charts compare targets. Over the next 60 days, ask others for tips on how they create graphs and visual images. Then, incorporate charts and graphs in your presentations and reports. Ask for feedback from those who are reviewing your work. Keep track of your efforts, learnings, and outcomes based on your work in this area.

- **Review presentations that have persuaded others.** One of the most effective ways to improve your use of data is to learn how others present it effectively. Google "examples of influential presentations," and review those from the most reputable sources, such as *Forbes*. Consider: What data is included in the presentation? How is the data presented? What data is not included? How are complex terms or scenarios explained? How are the needs of the audience taken into account? Make note of the best practices you see as well as your overall conclusions. If possible, meet with people who regularly make presentations and discuss best practices they use when creating their presentations. Determine how you will incorporate these tactics into your own approach. Make a commitment to do this within the next 30 to 60 days. Keep track of your work in this area, and share your learnings with your manager or a peer.

- **Spend time learning about data analysis tools and how to use them (for example, Microsoft Excel or SAS).** Start with programs such as Microsoft Excel or SAS; take the tutorials to learn how this tool can help you make decisions. Practice the techniques you learn with small decisions. As you build comfort, allow these types of tools to take a bigger role in your data analysis and decision-making process. Put this approach into action for the next 60 days. Make note of your learnings and the outcomes.

- **Network with or meet with someone who works in Marketing or R&D (Research and Development) or Sales about how they analyze and use data.** Research people in your network on LinkedIn or ask others who they know who works in one of these areas. Meet with this person within the next 30 days. Ask what data they believe is most important in their work. How do they analyze the data? What do they do with imperfect data? How do they work around data that is unavailable? Ask about the conclusions, recommendations, and predictions they make. Ask them to review a few of the more recent, data-based decisions they've made. What were the outcomes of those decisions? Make note of the themes and concepts that resonate the most with you, and keep a list of the tactics that you can incorporate into your own approach.

- **Read books that help you learn how to gather and leverage data.** Suggestions include:
  - *Competitive Intelligence: How to Gather, Analyze, and Use Information to Move Your Business to the Top* by Larry Kahaner
  - *Data Modeling Made Simple: A Practical Guide for Business and IT Professionals* by Steve Hoberman

○ *Information Dashboard Design: The Effective Visual Communication of Data* by Stephen Few

Dedicate at least 30 minutes a week to reading these resources. For a period of 60 days, make note of the things you learn and new things you would like to try. Review these with your manager or a trusted peer. Discuss how you can incorporate these learnings into your routine.

Ideas for leveraging:

- **Conduct one-on-one or small group training sessions about different topics related to analyzing data.** Examples include:
  ○ Leveraging data analysis tools
  ○ Influencing with data
  ○ Balancing data analysis with analysis paralysis
  ○ Using data to make better decisions

- **Select issues and examples that you feel passionate about.** Encourage two-way communication. Make it relevant by asking the attendees for examples of decisions they need to make. Keep track of the work you do and the impact it seems to have on others.

- **Develop a short presentation reviewing your approach to finding and analyzing data.** Include tips, best practices, resources, and real-world examples or cases to showcase your experience and knowledge. Host a virtual or in-person training session with people who want to improve in this area. As an alternative, share your presentation online: Shoot a short video and post it on YouTube, or create a PowerPoint presentation and post it on your own blog, or on another platform.

- **Coach people who want to learn how to better synthesize data.** Help them determine their specific areas to improve, and discuss what hinders them from doing more in this area. Talk about best practices, tools, technology, and research. Share concrete suggestions for how to get better in this area. If appropriate, have them observe you for a period of time. Meet with them regularly to review their progress.

- **Offer to lend your skills in data analysis to a project team.** Help a cross-functional team or a special task force responsible for driving important results. Offer to help it gather, analyze, and leverage data to build the business case for change. Keep track of the work you do and the impact it seems to have on others.

Behavior 5: Takes Calculated Risks

When is taking a risk a good idea? How big of a risk is too big? People who take calculated risks can take action despite ambiguous circumstances or incomplete information. They show good judgment in balancing the need for information with the need for action.

Ideas for improving this skill:

- **Know your limits.** When it comes to taking calculated risks, it's important to have clear guidelines about what risks lie too far outside of your comfort zone. Make a list of your limitations or non-negotiables when it comes to taking risks. Examples might include:

  - Situations in which the risk outweighs the reward
  - Violating conduct codes or ethical standards
  - Losing past a certain dollar amount
  - Violating your values or set priorities
  - Potentially hurting others

  After you develop your personal list, share it with a trusted friend and ask for feedback. Adjust the list accordingly and leverage it when working through risk-related decisions for the next 60 days. Note how it impacts your ability to take responsible risk. Share your learnings and outcomes with your manager or a mentor.

- **When faced with a risk-related decision, make yourself a checklist to help you consider important criteria related to the decision:**

  - Will it have minimal impact on current operations?
  - Have you incorporated and considered all the data you have? Is it consistent with your values?

- What is the best-case scenario? What is the worst-case scenario?

- How could this decision impact your career positively? Negatively?

- Can it be realistically implemented with your current resources?

Put this approach into action when making decisions for the next 30 days. Track the results of the risks you take, and reflect with a peer or your manager about how your checklist questions impacted the results.

- **To make sure you have analyzed all important information in your decision making, create a decision-making template that includes the following:**

  - Definition of the problem

  - Important and critical facts that are known

  - Important information that is missing, and how you can obtain it

  - How do those impacted feel about the problem or issue?

  - Are there related problems that will be affected by this decision?

  - What are the long- and short-term consequences to this decision?

Try this approach for the next five significant decisions you have to make. Ask a trusted adviser, or your manager, to review your thought process. Keep track of the outcomes of your decisions, what you learned, and what you would do differently.

- **Pilot new ideas and initiatives.** To build your ability to take risks, try new ideas on a small scale, testing the results of your efforts. Over the next 60 days, develop a set of metrics that you'll use to evaluate success, and why it might succeed or fail. Measure the success of the initiative. What new ideas develop as a result of these efforts? What would you do differently next time? Would you try your idea again, just in slightly different conditions? What creative ways of thinking emerge? After you complete your analysis and conclusions about the success of your effort, share your learnings with trusted colleagues or friends.

- **Adopt formal methods and processes for making decisions and leveraging stronger judgment.** For the next 30 days, spend 1 hour per week learning about new-to-you strategies to assess risk, and record what you find. These might include

  ○ Decision trees

  ○ Grid Analysis

  ○ Fishbone diagramming

  ○ Cost benefit analysis

  ○ SWOT Analysis

  ○ Six Thinking Hats

  ○ Probability and Statistical Thinking Analysis

  Practice implementing these techniques when you make daily decisions. Self-evaluate after your implementation. Did it make your decisions easier? Was it the most efficient and effective way for you to measure risk? How could it have been better? Consider building a list of your favorite tools and techniques and sharing with friends or your manager.

- **Seek feedback and buy-in for important decisions.** When faced with a high-risk decision, seek buy-in from those the risk would affect. Take it a step further by thinking outside of your comfort zone to identify individuals who might benefit from inclusion in this project. During each conversation, share the information that you have, the potential risk that you foresee, as well as the potential gain. Solicit input and recommendations and ask for their buy-in. After each conversation, reflect on how the conversation/buy-in impacted your willingness to take on the risk. Put this approach into action for the next 60 days.

- **Talk with people who manage risk regularly.** Over the next 30 days, schedule time to interview individuals who successfully take calculated risk on a regular basis. Ask them questions like, What is your approach to taking responsible risks? What factors do you consider when taking risks? What tools do you leverage to navigate the process? How do you deal with limited information? How do you manage anxiety? Can you share an example of a time when taking responsible risks positively impacted you? What did you learn? Can you share an example of a time when taking responsible risks negatively impacted you? What did you learn? Record your findings and identify at least three specific tools and techniques that you plan to implement going forward.

To take it further, ask one of these individuals to provide you with guidance on a specific decision you are facing in a situation with limited information. Share the problem, the potential solutions, and ask her to weigh in. Take notes regarding her advice. Make notes of the themes and concepts that resonate the most with you, and keep a list of the things you plan on incorporating into your approach.

Commit to implementing this plan within the next 30 to 60 days, and share your learnings and outcomes with your manager or a trusted advisor.

- **Dealing with limited information, map out the best-case/worst-case scenarios.** Taking calculated risks is deeply connected to making decisions with limited information. Next time you are in this situation, look at both sides of the decision (that is, "go" or "no-go"). For each side, write down the best-case scenario and the worst-case scenario given the information you have. Compare the scenarios. Does either scenario seem too risky? Does either scenario have limited upside? Put this approach into action when making decisions for the next 60 days. Later, share your learnings and outcomes with your manager or a colleague.

- **Learn as much as you can about what defines success with respect to taking calculated risks.** Ask your manager to help set expectations and articulate how outcomes are measured, with an eye toward how you should approach risk. Ask for specific examples of successful approaches to risk and less successful approaches to risk. Record your findings and use it to help you build a definition for taking responsible risks. Review your definition regularly when making decisions and update it as needed. Put this approach into action for the next 30 days.

Later, share your learnings and outcomes with your manager or a mentor.

- **Try "easing into" the decision.** When pushed to make decisions with limited information, mitigate the risk by breaking your large decision down into smaller, more manageable decisions. Are there any smaller, more immediate decisions that you can make to help you learn more about or feel out the situation? Are there any first-step decisions that are worth pursuing before making a final decision? How about second-step decisions? Put this approach into action for the next 30 days and reflect on how it helps you take responsible risk. Share your learnings and outcomes with your manager or a friend.

- **Regularly conduct a "post mortem" on risky decisions and judgment calls.** Compare the results to your intentions or predictions and identify the gaps. What went well? What did not go well? Why? What information do you have now that you did not have then? Ask others who were involved with or impacted by a decision you made for feedback. What did they think went well? What could have been done differently? For each decision, identify two specific things you would do again and two things you would do differently. Document these conversations, learnings, and conclusions. Recognize and learn from both victories and failures. Keep track of your work in this area over the next 30 to 60 days, and share your learnings with your manager or a trusted advisor.

- **Read books that inspire taking risk and living with the results.** Suggestions include:
  - *You Unstuck: Mastering the New Rules of Risk-Taking at Work and in Life* by Libby Gill
  - *Celebrating Failure: The Power of Taking Risks, Making Mistakes and Thinking Big* by Ralph Heath
  - *Risk Intelligence: How to Live with Uncertainty* by Dylan Evans

  Dedicate at least 30 minutes a week to reading the resources you choose. For a period of 60 days, make note of the things you learn and new things you would like to try. Review these with your manager or a trusted peer. Discuss how you can incorporate these learnings into your routine.

Ideas for leveraging:

- **Conduct one-on-one or small group training sessions about different topics in taking responsible risk, such as**
  - Risk versus reward analysis
  - Seeking feedback and buy-in
  - Leveraging tools and processes

  Keep track of the work you do and the impact it seems to have on others.

- **Host a virtual or live lunch-n-learn to discuss common problems others face in taking calculated risks.** Prepare a discussion around what it means to take responsible risk. Use past examples of successes and failures and encourage the audience members to do the same. Share tips and advice and recommend small action steps to help others improve. Keep track of the work you do and the impact it seems to have on others.

- **Develop a short presentation reviewing your approach to taking responsible risk.** Include tips, best practices, resources, and real-world examples or cases to showcase your experience and knowledge. Host a virtual or in-person training session with people who want to improve in this area. As an alternative, share your presentation online: Shoot a short video and post it on YouTube, or create a PowerPoint presentation and post it on your own blog or on another platform. Keep track of your work in this area.

- **Help others who struggle in this area by documenting your decision making process through a simple decision tree model or flow chart.** Show how one piece of information leads to another and how answers to pivotal questions determine your next step. Illustrating the process like this can help others learn a new way to approach their own decision making.

3

Competency: Engages and Develops People

Behavior 1: Builds Trusted Relationships
Behavior 2: Influences Others
Behavior 3: Promotes Teamwork

Overview of Competency

Having great people skills and knowing how to engage and develop those around you is critical to success in any career or workplace. People who engage and develop others establish and nurture relationships of mutual trust and respect with those around them. They know how to build and lead teams successfully by communicating with warmth and clarity. They coach and inspire others to achieve and grow and view the selection of talent to be of critical importance. They actively support and guide the development of team members and others. They know everyone has something of value to contribute and seek out a diversity of talents. They persuasively influence others and model collaboration.

Behavior 1: Builds Trusted Relationships

Think of a friend or co-worker with whom you enjoy working. What are the qualities of your relationship with that person that make it enjoyable to work together? Someone who builds trusted relationships actively develops, maintains, and invests in relationships that inspire trust and mutual respect. They build enduring "win-win" partnerships and model exceptional two-way communication skills.

Ideas for improving this skill:

- **Assess the quality of your relationships.** Over the next 30 days, list the primary relationships you have with friends, family, co-workers, and mentors. Assess how successful each relationship is by answering the following questions in writing:

  - Are our discussions usually one-way or two-way?
  - How often do we exchange ideas?
  - How often do I ask questions of this person?
  - Do I learn from this person?
  - Does this person learn from me?
  - How does this relationship benefit each of us?

  Use your answers to rate the success of each relationship on a scale of 1 to 5. For those relationships receiving the lowest rating, choose the three that are your top priority. Then create a plan to increase your rapport, appreciation, and positive interactions with these people. Review your plan with your manager or a trusted advisor and then implement it and track your activity and learnings over the next 30 days.

- **Actively build personal rapport throughout your relationships.** Over the next 60 days, make it a point to learn more about the people around you. Learn and track information that is relevant to that person. What shapes their beliefs? Where are they coming from? Take notes about your friends, colleagues, and others, and store that information for later. Share information about yourself when appropriate. Keep track of your work in building these relationships so that you can refer to it again.

- **Find more opportunities to connect with those around you.** Look for ways to connect with friends and co-workers, and create new opportunities to get to know them better. Schedule meetings, lunches, coffee breaks, and more to help build your network and better understand the needs of those around you. For the next 2 months, schedule one of these interactions every week. Keep notes about how your relationships are changing and how these changes benefit both you and the other person. At the end of the 2-month period, review your progress and learnings with your manager or a mentor. Set a new goal for continuing to build your network in a meaningful way.

- **Keep track of issues in your relationships.** Make a list of the most common obstacles you've encountered with friends, peers, and co-workers. These may include uncertainty about who's supposed to be doing what, lack of consistent communication, and so on. Review this list with your manager or a trusted advisor. How can you be more proactive to avoid these same obstacles in your future interactions? Commit to acting upon their advice for the next 30 days. Track your progress and share your learnings with your manager or advisor.

- **Encourage two-way communication in your relationships.** Build opportunities to gather feedback about your communication to improve your relationships. Some ideas include:
  o Ask for comments and questions (along with the means of responding) at the end of email messages.
  o Ask for opinions and feedback from those around you about your work on joint projects or events.
  o After listening to someone, see if you can repeat back to them what you heard. Ask, "Am I understanding you correctly? Is this what you meant?"

  Be sure to address or act on the feedback that you collect. For the next 30 days, try different methods of soliciting feedback to see which feel most comfortable to you. Keep track of your efforts and review your progress with your manager or a trusted friend.

- **Show people that you value them during interactions.** Over the next 30 days, try one or more of these techniques to show others that you genuinely value them.
  o *Record, remember, and recall information about people.* When meeting people for the first time, repeat their name at least three times in the conversation to help ensure that you remember it. During your conversation ask them about something unique to them, such as where they grew up or who they cheered for in the Super Bowl. When you get back

to your office, put the information you've gathered in your contacts list. The next time you see them, recall the information from the last conversation and build on the conversation.

o *Give people your full attention.* Commit to staying completely attuned when others share information with you. Close your computer and put your phone down during these interactions. Look people in the eye, nod to show understanding, and try to reframe and repeat the messages you hear.

o *Ask people how they are doing.* Ask questions like, How's it going? Is everything all right? Look them in the eye, wait for their response, and then acknowledge it. When possible, offer a suggestion and your assistance to help them out. Record what you learn about each individual and how you responded.

- **Convey your trustworthiness by your actions.** People pay attention to what you do more than what you say, so show them that you are trustworthy. Over the next 30 days, take extra steps to build trust with those around you. Following are some guidelines:

o *Keep your promises.* Do what you say you are going to do, and meet your deadlines.

o *Keep it to yourself.* If someone has told you something in confidence, do not share it with anyone. (If it is something that may be potentially damaging to a person or the organization, tell the person that you feel obligated to tell your manager or HR, or encourage them to do so.)

o *Offer to help.* Pitch in with last-minute deadlines, special issues, or sudden emergencies.

o *Send a quick congratulatory note* to someone who deserves it. Acknowledge their victory. Recognize their contribution.

These steps can help you develop a reputation as someone who is reliable and helpful.

- *Read books that provide insight into developing and sustaining trusting relationship.* Suggestions include:
  - *Emotional Intelligence 2.0* by Travis Bradberry and Jean Greaves
  - *People Tools: 54 Strategies for Building Relationships, Creating Joy, and Embracing Prosperity* by Alan C. Fox
  - *The SPEED of Trust: The One Thing That Changes Everything* by Stephen M.R. Covey

  Dedicate at least 30 minutes a week to reading these resources. For a period of 60 days, make note of the things you learn and new things you would like to try. Review these with your manager or a trusted peer. Discuss how you can incorporate these learnings into your routine.

Ideas for leveraging:

- **Coach someone who struggles with building relationships.** Review your approach to making and nurturing your relationships with the purpose of sharing your approach with others. Observe people during interactions with others, and identify places where they could have taken a better approach. Learn about their fears, help them determine their biggest areas of opportunity, and suggest your ideas for improvement. Meet with them throughout the process to review their thoughts and concerns. Keep track of your activities and learnings in this area.

- **Host a virtual or live lunch-n-learn to discuss the importance of partnerships.** Prepare a discussion around developing strong partnerships and ways to build trust, share information, and identify others' needs. Use past examples of successes and failures and encourage others to do the same. Share tips and advice and recommend small action steps to help others practice and improve.

- **Develop a short presentation to teach relationship and partnership skills.** Include tips, best practices, resources, and real-world examples or cases to showcase your experience and knowledge. Topics could include being approachable, active listening, and showing respect for others. Host a virtual or in-person training session with people who want to improve in this area. As an alternative, share your presentation online: Shoot a short video and post it online, or create a PowerPoint presentation and post it on your blog or on another platform.

Behavior 2: Influences Others

Have you had a goal that required others' participation? What did you do to bring them onboard to work with you? People who are skilled at influencing others have the ability to build consensus by persuading others. They gain cooperation from others to accomplish their goals and have credibility among peers and managers. They are adept at negotiating to achieve their desired outcomes.

Ideas for improving this skill:

- **Think of "trading" and "understanding" as currency when influencing without authority.** Doing so helps you identify common ground and mutual benefits before entering a conversation.
  - *Trading.* When you want something from people, prepare by thinking about what they want or need and identify how you can help them accomplish their goals.
  - *Understanding.* Think about what you're asking for and try to anticipate beforehand how it will impact them; work to identify common ground and mutual benefits before entering the conversation.

  Over the next 30 days, practice conversing with others while using these concepts. Reflect on what went differently about the conversation, how effective it was, and what you learned. Track your efforts in this area, and share your learnings with your manager or a trusted friend.

- **Connect with people on a more personal level.** Strong relationships are extremely helpful when trying to influence others. Over the next 30 days, make personal connections a priority in every interaction. Concentrate on learning details regarding others' background and hobbies, and try to find mutual interests. Use this information to build rapport early in the relationship and a conversation. Keep track of your work in this area, and determine how you can build a mutually beneficial relationship with each person. After 30 days, share what you've observed with your manager or a peer.

- **Prepare to influence by utilizing four well-known techniques:**

  - *Prepare the WIFM (What's In It For Me).* Before you approach someone whom you'd like to influence, take time to identify the WIFM on both sides. The more you can do to point out what's in it for them, the more influential you will be.

  - Go into conversations with *a clear idea of what you want.* Write out your request beforehand and practice getting your messaging down to a sentence or two. Creating true clarity about your needs and wants is the first step to influencing.

  - *Know your audience.* Each person is motivated by a different factor (for example, job challenge, learning new things, accomplishing something worthwhile, autonomy, pay, and praise). The more you know about the people you want to influence, the more you will understand how to influence them. Talk with someone you trust to learn more about the person you'd like to influence.

  - *Support your desired outcomes with research, facts, and data.* Practice linking your requests to the available information. Showcase this information when persuading and influencing others.

Later, consider the outcomes of these conversations and how comfortable you felt with these new techniques. Make note of which worked the best for you and which resulted in the outcome you were seeking. What would you do differently next time? Track your efforts over the next 60 days and then share your learnings with your manager or a trusted mentor.

- **Focus on mutual benefits to ensure a constructive, not manipulative, approach.** Try these techniques:

  - View the person that you are dealing with as a peer, rather than a target.

o Spend ample time and energy thinking about the mutual benefits associated with a good outcome.

o Take time to visit and connect with the people whom you'd like to influence. Ask their opinions about your position, and gather their ideas and reactions.

Over the next 60 days, practice conversing with others keeping these concepts in mind. Reflect on what went differently about the conversation, how effective it was, and what you learned. Track your efforts in this area, and share your learnings with your manager or a friend.

- **Create a specific and organized approach to influencing difficult people.** Approach each of their arguments as an opportunity to give them something they need. Try these tips:

  o Prepare for the interaction by listing their potential concerns and arguments and then developing responses that reflect a shared agenda and a willingness to help them get what they need.

  o Do not reject their dissenting opinions. Instead, try on their point of view without agreeing or disagreeing. Be sincerely curious about their stance and try to determine the principles behind it.

  o When you stand up to others, begin by assuming they mean well and acknowledge their good intentions: (such as "I appreciate that you want the project to be successful. I have another way to look at what we need to do.") This method allows you to get your point across without overriding or disrespecting the other person's opinion.

Over the next 30 days, keep track of the instances in which you put these approaches into action. Make note of your learnings and the outcomes. Share your insights with your manager or a peer.

- **Influence others by being more assertive.** Try one of these techniques:

  o Study how assertive people start discussions, deal with interruptions, express their views, and respond to criticism.

o Practice clearly stating your point of view directly and confidently, especially when you're in safe environments, interacting with those close to you.

o Pay attention to how you feel when you ask for what you want. Note the difference in how other people treat you when you are assertive. Use these reflections to motivate yourself to continue to assert yourself.

o Say no when you need to; don't procrastinate or appear tentative. Monitor your nonverbal actions to make sure they are in alignment with your words. (Make eye contact, stand up straight, and so on.)

For the next 30 days, try at least once a week to assert yourself. Keep track of when you try these tips, both within and outside of work, and review this with your manager or a trusted friend.

- **Identify an influential person and ask them to mentor you.** Observe them in social situations, pull out key behaviors and characteristics, and model these behaviors in your own interactions. Ask about their approach and technique for influencing and handling difficult people. If appropriate, ask this person to introduce you to influential members of their network. Take notes regarding their advice. Make notes of the themes and concepts that resonate the most with you, and keep a list of the things you plan on incorporating into your approach. Share your learnings regularly with this person or your manager.

- **Build a broader network to influence others more effectively.** Build a broad network of relationships with people you need to be successful. Leverage your network to make connections with people you want to influence. If you do not personally know someone that you'd like to influence, find someone in your network to help make the personal connection. Utilize LinkedIn and other social media to help you. After the connection has been made, use your mutual connection to build common ground and establish trust. Offer to do the same for others. Keep track of your work in this area over the next 30 days, and share your learnings with your manager or a mentor.

- **Read books that provide useful advice for influencing and persuading others.** Suggestions include:
  - *The Skinny on the Art of Persuasion: How to Move Minds* by Jim Randel
  - *Talk Less, Say More: Three Habits to Influence Others and Make Things Happen* by Connie Dieken
  - *Influence: The Psychology of Persuasion* by Robert B. Cialdini

  Dedicate at least 30 minutes a week to reading these resources. For a period of 60 days, make note of the things you learn and new things you would like to try. Review these with your manager or a trusted peer. Discuss how you can incorporate these learnings into your routine.

Ideas for leveraging:

- **Coach someone who would like to build their influencing skills.** Review your approach to negotiating for what you want. Share with them your own tips for assessing your audience and determining the win-win opportunity. Observe them in interactions with others, and identify places where they could be more persuasive.

  Meet with them over a period of several weeks. Assess how effectively you coach, and share your activities and learnings with your manager over time.

- **Develop a short presentation on the art of influencing.** Include tips, best practices, resources, and real-world examples and cases to showcase your experience and knowledge. Topics may include:
  - "What's In It For Me"
  - Building a strong network
  - Negotiating for what you want

  Host a virtual or in-person training session with people who want to develop their skills in this area. As an alternative, share your presentation online: Film a short video and post it on You-Tube, or create a PowerPoint presentation and post it on your own blog or on another platform.

- **Host a virtual or live lunch-n-learn to discuss influencing techniques.** Prepare a discussion around influencing without authority. Share past examples of successes and failures and encourage others to do the same. Share tips and advice and recommend small action steps to help others practice and improve.

- **Conduct one-on-one or small group training sessions about influencing.** Ideas include:
  - Gaining others' trust
  - The give-and-take of negotiating
  - Building a strong network

  Keep track of your activities and the impact they seem to have on others.

Behavior 3: Promotes Teamwork

Think back to your best experiences working as part of a team in either your personal or professional life. What helped make your best team experience successful? People who promote teamwork collaborate well with others to achieve goals. They actively break down barriers between team members and identify and share best practices with others. They create a sense of unity and purpose among team members.

Ideas for improving this skill:

- **Educate yourself about teams.** If you tend to dislike working on teams, perhaps you've never been on an effective one before. Within the next 30 days, do some research to discover the characteristics of effective teams. These include clear roles and responsibilities, shared vision, consistent methods of communication, and regular check-in times. Ask yourself, Which of these characteristics was missing in my past team experiences? How did that affect the outcome? How can I help ensure these guidelines are in place the next time I am on a team? Make notes of your answers, so you can share these the next time you're on a team.

- **Encourage others to share their ideas.** On an effective team, people feel comfortable sharing and debating new ideas. You can show team members that you value their input by trying these techniques:
  - Validating what someone else says before adding your ideas
  - Welcoming idea fragments as much as complete plans
  - Saying "and" instead of "but" when responding to suggestions
  - Publicly acknowledging previous ideas that have been successful
  - Listening attentively to what your team members are saying

  Commit to putting these five simple tips into action over the next 30 days. Note how people react to your efforts. Share your progress with your manager or a trusted friend.

- **Build and work from a shared agenda.** Think about how your needs align with those of each member of your team. What do you both stand to gain from a positive relationship? What desired outcomes do you share? What desired outcomes conflict? Document this information and refer to it when working together. Think through the conflicts before key interactions and reference the aligned priorities often. Use this approach for the next 30-60 days and keep track of your efforts. Make note of any feedback you get, and what learnings you can glean from the outcomes.

- **Help team members succeed.** Take time to identify what people on your team need to be successful and what challenges they are anticipating. Over the next 60 days, regularly solicit input about what your team members are concerned about and identify ways that you can help. If you can't help, think about someone who can help and make the connection on behalf of your teammate. Take this a step further by hosting a forum where team members share challenges and ways to work through or around them. Later, share your learnings and outcomes with your manager or a mentor.

- **Actively build rapport to foster collaboration and openness.** Strong relationships are critical to successful teamwork. Over the next 60 days, make extra efforts to connect with your team members on a personal level.

○ Learn details regarding their background. Find mutual interests, and use this information to build rapport. File away the personal level information that you learn so that you can refer to it the next time you see them.

○ When appropriate, share personal information about yourself. Let your partners get to know you as you are also learning about them.

Keep track of your work in building and leveraging this cache of personal information to strengthen your relationships. Share your learnings with your manager or a trusted friend.

• **Encourage and host social gatherings.** Help facilitate some time for team members to get to know one another. Over the next 30 days, schedule at least one social event for the team. Maybe an informal happy hour? Maybe a team coffee break? Augment this by inviting team members out to lunch or coffee when possible. Use this time to get to know each individual and be sure to share information about yourself. At the end of the month, reflect on how the additional investment of time impacts collaboration among your teammates.

• **Collaborate on a project outside of your comfort zone.** Over the next 30-60 days, listen for and actively seek out instances to collaborate with others on a project or effort that differs from your usual interests. Find a group that is struggling with a problem and offer your services. Find out what you can add to the group. Do you have a skill set that they would find useful? Can you bring different experiences to the table? Find a way to contribute to a group that you would not otherwise be involved with and help them resolve their problem. Later, take note of your experiences: Who did you enjoy working with and why? What did you learn? What effort will you take to maintain this new network? Share your experiences with your manager or a mentor or coach.

• **Offer to facilitate a brainstorming session.** Identify the team you will help within the next 30-60 days. Prior to the session, meet with the team and agree on the outcomes for the session by identifying what they want to accomplish. Plan and prepare for the meeting by including facilitation tactics that will encourage participants to actively participate and share ideas. During the session, take the lead in ensuring effective communication and collaboration. Work to make sure that everyone's opinion is heard and all perspectives are carefully considered. Encourage participants to brainstorm ideas, build on one another's input, and develop solutions that consider a wide variety of perspectives and inputs. Afterward, ask for feedback on the session. What went well? What could have gone better? Did everyone share? Did the final outcomes reflect a wide variety of opinions? Record the themes that emerged and make a plan to be more successful going forward. If possible, facilitate a follow-up meeting with your new learnings in mind and reflect on how you improved. Later, share your learnings and outcomes with your manager or a trusted advisor.

- **Share your knowledge, and ask for help.** Improve your collaboration skills by demonstrating regular give-and-take. Over the next 60 days, practice helping others and sharing your expertise when they need it. On the reverse side, discuss your own projects and obstacles and solicit ideas from others. Don't be afraid to ask for help. Show that you have the right balance of initiative, flexibility, and receptivity to be a valuable member of the team. Record your efforts and make note of how people react and reciprocate. Share your progress with your manager or a friend.

- **Read books that inspire innovative and creative problem solving strategies for teams.** Suggestions include:
  - *The 17 Indisputable Laws of Teamwork: Embrace Them and Empower Your Team* by John C. Maxwell
  - *High Five! The Magic of Working Together* by Ken Blanchard and Sheldon Bowles
  - *Team Players and Teamwork, Completely Updated and Revised: New Strategies for Developing Successful Collaboration* by Glenn M. Parker
  - *The Five Dysfunctions of a Team: A Leadership Fable* by Patrick Lencioni

Dedicate at least 30 minutes a week to reading these resources. For a period of 60 days, make note of the things you learn and new things you would like to try. Review these with your manager or a trusted peer. Discuss how you can incorporate these learnings into your routine.

Ideas for leveraging:

- **Coach someone who struggles to be an effective team member.** Begin by reviewing the top essential guidelines for effective teams. Watch them during team interactions, and give them immediate feedback on what they can do better. Offer to role-play common scenarios that come up when working with teams. Guide them through the steps of effective communication and give-and-take. Encourage them to commit to making two or three changes to their approach based on your advice and feedback. Check in with them afterward to see how they're doing, and give them feedback based on what you observe.

- **Develop a workshop that teaches teamwork.** Agenda items should include:
  - Supporting the team's mission
  - Understanding, and acting upon, clear roles and responsibilities
  - The importance of co-creating guiding principles for the team
  - Communicating consistently
  - Allowing for everyone's input
  - Adhering to timelines, check-ins, and milestones

- **Host a virtual or in-person training session with people who want to improve in this area.** As an alternative, share your presentation online: Shoot a short video and post it on YouTube, or create a PowerPoint presentation and post it on your own blog or on another platform. Keep track of your activities in this area and the feedback from your attendees.

- **Host a virtual or live lunch-n-learn to discuss best practices in teamwork.** Prepare a discussion around the basic ingredients for an effective team, as well as common obstacles to team success. Use examples of your own past team challenges and how you overcame them. Keep track of the work you do and the impact it has on others.

- **Develop and share teamwork templates.** Document your best practices for effective teams, including
  - Project objectives and guiding principles
  - Definitions of roles
  - Project plans with milestones and check-ins
  - Sample team meeting agendas
  - Sample team communication schedules

Find a way to share these templates and best practices, either through a blog or by speaking at other groups' events.

4

Competency: Delivers Results

Behavior 1: Demonstrates Business Acumen

Behavior 2: Champions Customer Focus

Behavior 3: Plans and Organizes

Behavior 4: Sets and Drives Priorities

Behavior 5: Overcomes Obstacles

Behavior 6: Demonstrates Technological Savvy

Overview of Competency

At the end of the day, one of the most important abilities people must have to succeed in a workplace is the ability to deliver results. People who can deliver results marshal resources to get things done. They demonstrate a consistently high level of customer focus and clearly understand the link between customer satisfaction and delivering organizational results. They stay on track, even when presented with barriers and setbacks. They measure performance against priorities and evaluate outcomes. Above all, they are action-oriented and not fearful of acting, even with unclear or incomplete information.

Behavior 1: Demonstrates Business Acumen

What does it mean to have *business acumen*? People with business acumen understand and leverage economic, financial, customer, and industry information. They can see the big picture and comprehend the structure, logistics, and flow of the organization. They know how their area and their work supports their organization's overall goals and its customers.

Ideas for improving this skill:

- **Keep up with your business and industry news (or for the industry you want to join).** Find a resource that resonates with you (for example, business blogs, *Fast Company*, *Wall Street Journal*, *The New York Times*, and *The Economist*) delivered in a mode that fits your lifestyle (such as a podcast, mobile app, or magazine). In particular, make it your business to:

  - **Learn about industry trends.** Who are the most-talked about organizations and why? What are the hot products and services? What economic issues are affecting your industry and why?

  - **Focus on new technologies.** How is emerging technology affecting your industry? What will customers expect from organizations as technology makes access faster and easier? What skills and talents will organizations need to grow or acquire over the next 24 months?

  - **Pick your favorite organization and learn about its competition.** Read its competitors' websites, annual reports, and earnings statements. Look for commonalities and key differences.

  - **Set up Google alerts to receive key industry information.** Sign up for alerts about your favorite organization, competitors, key products, or services. For at least 1 month, assess the information you receive and adjust your settings to hone in on the most value-added information.

  - **Learn about macro-economic indicators and trends.** Obtain a basic understanding of the big picture numbers watched closely by engaged business people.

  Keep track of your key business findings for, initially, 30 days, and discuss your observations and questions with your peers each month. Consider passing along pertinent learnings to peers and others interested in your industry of choice.

- **Ask someone knowledgeable about organizational finance for a tutorial.** Over the next 30 to 60 days, learn about the following in order to gain a better understanding of what makes an organization tick:

o An organization's year-to-date (or most recent) Profit & Loss statement if available. For a private company, review the information made available to employees. Assess what most affects revenue, costs, and profitability. Determine key levers and business cycles for driving quarterly or annual profit (or other key deliverable).

o Which metrics evaluate the organization externally? How are they calculated (for example, using EBITDA, which is a common measure of profitability)?

o How is the performance of the different work units assessed? How can these metrics fit into the metrics of the organization?

o What are the greatest financial risks expected over the next 24 to 36 months? How is the organization likely to manage them?

Take notes as you learn. Review them on a regular basis until these metrics and reports are familiar to you. Test yourself by reading key financial reports, and then check your understanding with your tutor.

• **If possible, shadow someone as her department undergoes the annual budgeting process.** Understand how organizational goals and the budgeting process mutually help define one another through discussion. Keep the following questions in mind as you participate:

o What data is used to set and evaluate the strategic priorities of the department?

o How is budget development directly linked to corporate strategy?

o How are capital and operating resources strategically allocated? (Ask to see the capital and operating budgets if you do not have them.)

o What performance measures will be put into place to monitor progress toward the strategic goals?

o How will cost management efforts be linked to the budget?

○ What flexibility does the budget offer if priorities need to change?

Take detailed notes and document your questions. Later share your learnings and your questions with your manager or a trusted advisor.

- **Pick an organization in your industry of choice and learn about its value chain and the different roles in it.** Over the next 30 to 60 days, gather information to determine the answers to questions like the following:

  ○ How does the organization make money?

  ○ Who are its customers?

  ○ What affects its buying decisions?

  ○ What does the business do to ensure high levels of customer service?

  ○ What is at stake if each group within it doesn't drive results or partner strategically with the business?

  Keep track of your learnings over 30 days and review all you've learned and your analysis with your manager or a trusted friend.

- **Learn about the challenges and opportunities faced by an organization's leaders.** If possible, get time with a leader in an organization you admire within the next 60 days. Let her know that you want to understand the challenges she experiences and opportunities she sees in the organization over a cup of coffee or a meeting in her office. Ask questions like, "What industry trends represent the greatest opportunity for your organization? What presents the biggest risk to you? Where do you see your organization as a leader? Where are you lagging? What will be the most important skills and experiences for employees to have in the future?" Make note of her answers and discuss your findings with your manager or a peer.

- **Interview a forward-thinking leader about how to spot industry trends.** Within the next 30 days, identify a leader in an organization whom you believe has his eyes on upcoming trends in his industry. Reach out to him for coffee and ask how he spots trends. What are the signs? When does a "phase" become a legitimate trend? And how can employees best capitalize on a trend when they see one? What will be the most important skills and experiences for employees to have in the future? Make notes during the conversation, and later analyze what you learned. Share your learnings with your manager or an advisor.

- **Pick your favorite organization and study its competition's successes and failures.** When you work for an organization, knowing about your competition is key to understanding your own company. A good way to learn how the competition thinks is to study how it handles success and failure. Over the next 30 days, look back at the 2 or 3 successes and failures for each of the competitors. For each one, ask questions like, Why was this initiative successful? Unsuccessful? How did it further leverage its success? How did it mitigate its failures? How did its offerings change after each success? After each failure? Discuss your learnings with your manager or a trusted advisor.

- **Practice documenting the work you do and receiving feedback from customers.** If you aren't in a workplace, think about "customers" as people in your life to whom you have responsibilities. Maybe it's your professors if you're in college or family members. From your point of view, clarify how things are working: roles and responsibilities of you versus your customers. What types of things delay or obstruct the way you work together? Document this information and review it with a trusted peer. Then, review it with your customers. With them, discuss what you can both do to improve your work together. Commit to implementing at least two ideas that come out of this process. Keep track of your activities, learnings, and progress over a period of 90 days and discuss your learnings with your manager or a mentor.

- **Understand and support the goals of those around you.** Over the next 30 to 60 days, make a special effort to get to know the goals of those around you, either at work or in your personal life. Ask questions about each person's background, experiences, priorities, and plans. Ask, What are your key goals? What changes do you anticipate this year? What are you most looking forward to? How can I help you reach your goals? Summarize their responses to them to ensure understanding. Take notes and determine what you can adjust or add to make sure you're supporting their goals. Review what you've learned and what actions you'll take with your manager or a friend.

- **Meet regularly with your customers to understand current and future needs.** Schedule regular conversations with customers for the next 3 to 6 months. (Again, this can be anyone in your life to whom you have responsibilities.) In the earlier conversations, ask probing questions to uncover their expectations and concerns, and be open to hearing the feedback. (Be sure to take detailed notes.) In the later conversations, identify the extent to which you are successfully meeting their needs based on the earlier conversations with an eye toward what you're doing well and what you could do even better. (Continue to log your insights from these conversations.) What themes and patterns emerge with respect to your performance? What will you do differently in the next 3 to 6 months? Keep track of your work in this area, and share your learnings with your manager or a trusted advisor.

- **Read books that provide guidance on enhancing one's own business acumen.** Suggestions include
  - *Seeing the Big Picture: Business Acumen to Build Your Credibility, Career, and Company* by Kevin Cope
  - *What the CEO Wants You to Know: How Your Company Really Works* by Ram Charan
  - *How to Read a Financial Report: Wringing Vital Signs Out of the Numbers* by John A. Tracy and Tage Tracy
  - *HBR's 10 Must Reads on Strategy* (including featured article "What is Strategy"? by Michael E. Porter and *Harvard Business Review*
  - *Competitive Strategy: Techniques for Analyzing Industries and Competitors* by Michael E. Porter

Dedicate at least 30 minutes a week to reading these resources. For a period of 60 days, make note of the things you learn and new things you would like to try. Review these with your manager or a trusted peer. Discuss how you can incorporate these learnings into your routine.

Ideas for leveraging:

- **Become a business coach.** For those interested in learning and reading more about your organization and business, show them what exists and help them find sources—and delivery modes—that fit their style. Show them how this information is relevant to the organization, their function, and their own role. Help them understand the business model, what the organization needs to do to stay alive, what key levers are used in operations, and how these impact the financial model. Help them understand the best ways to leverage their newfound knowledge in appropriate and value-added ways. Keep track of your efforts over several months and make note of your learnings and the impact it seems to have on others.

- **Share your industry and business knowledge via a short presentation.** Develop a presentation that shows others why keeping abreast of industry and economic trends is important. Highlight recent issues that affect the organization and your function. Share news stories and resources with others and explain why they're relevant. Host a virtual or in-person training session with people who want to develop their skills in this area. As an alternative, share your presentation online: Shoot a short video and post it on YouTube, or create a PowerPoint presentation and post it on your blog or on another platform.

- **Share tips about business happenings with your network.** As you come across relevant business information, news about your company or industry happenings, share it with people who would be most interested in or affected by it. Consider summarizing articles down to a few key sentences and adding a few bullet points regarding the importance or relevance of the information to your business. Do this for at least 3 months.

- **Become your team's *competition watch*.** Make it your business to keep track of your main competitors—their developments, their successes, and their challenges. Share your insights with your team on a regular basis, via a designated time during team meetings, email blasts, and more. Help your team understand how this information affects your organization and your team.

- **Help your team truly understand your organization's goals.** Offer to create a "speaker series" for your team consisting of leaders from different areas of the company. Ask the guests to talk about the priorities set for your organization and why they are important to the business. In addition, share financial and customer data and discuss the challenges your organization faces. Allow time for questions and answers.

Behavior 2: Champions Customer Focus

Being customer-focused can mean a variety of things, depending on how you define the word *customer*. The most obvious use of the term refers to customers to whom we're selling products and services. But if that doesn't apply to you, it could mean something else. For instance, if you work in a support function, such as Finance or Human Resources, it could mean customers within the organization: your "internal" customers. It could mean peers, fellow students—or truly anyone whose needs you are responsible for meeting. After you define your customer, *championing* them means consistently providing high customer service standards. People who do this see every customer interaction as an opportunity to leave a great impression. They actively seek to understand their customers' needs and recognize their own role in serving them. They do what it takes to ensure and exceed customer expectations. They understand the link between service and business results.

Ideas for improving this skill:

- **Document your process, roles, and service levels for your customers.** If you haven't already, clarify how things work from your vantage point, distinguish the roles and responsibilities of you versus those of your clients, and explain what types of things delay or obstruct your process. Document this information and review it with a trusted peer. Then, review it with your customers. With them, discuss: What can you both do to increase service and speed, or otherwise improve your work together? Commit to implementing at least two ideas that come out of this process. Keep track of your activities, learnings, and progress over a period of 90 days.

- **Encourage two-way communication with customers.** Build opportunities to gather customers' input to uncover and meet needs. Some ideas include:
  - Ask for comments and questions (along with the means of responding) at the end of email messages.
  - Allow time at the end of meeting agendas (face-to-face or virtual) to answer questions and listen to concerns.
  - Solicit opinions and feedback from your stakeholders via monthly phone calls or email messages.
  - Schedule a "gathering feedback" step in regular intervals of complicated, multifaceted communication plans.

  Be sure to address or act on the feedback that you collect. For the next 30 days, try different methods of soliciting feedback to see which feel most comfortable to you. Keep track of your efforts and review your progress with your manager or a mentor.

- **Meet regularly with your customers and ask them how you can add value.** Schedule regular conversations with customers for the next 3 to 6 months. In the earlier conversations, ask probing questions to uncover their expectations and concerns, and be open to hearing the feedback. (Be sure to take detailed notes.) In the later conversations, identify the extent to which you are successfully meeting their needs based on the earlier conversations with an eye toward what you're doing well and what you could do even better. (Continue to log your insights from these conversations.) What themes and patterns emerge with respect to your performance? What will you do differently in the next 3 to 6 months? Keep track of your work in this area, and share your learnings with your manager or a trusted advisor.

- **Ask for feedback from your clients and make it easy for them to give it to you.** You may never know if you don't ask. Create a set of questions to better understand the level of service you provide and the extent to which you meet and anticipate their needs. Questions might include:

- ○ How well am I meeting your needs?
- ○ Do you feel that problems and issues are resolved in a timely manner?
- ○ How satisfied are you with our communication?
- ○ What could I do differently to make our partnership more effective?
- ○ What would you like to see me do more often? Less often? If possible, make it easy for them to provide you with responses (for example, use a free survey tool such as Survey Monkey).

Make sure you react appropriately to the feedback, no matter how hard it is to hear—thank them for their comments and explain what you will do with them. For the next 60 days, keep track of your efforts as you collect feedback: Which questions were most effective? What did you learn? What actions did you take in response to these learnings? How did your relationships improve as a result of your increased responsiveness? Review your observations with your manager or a mentor and discuss ways to build ongoing feedback loops.

- **Ask yourself some tough questions about your service orientation.** Uncover your needs in this area by answering questions such as:
  - ○ What can I do today to follow through on a promise I've made?
  - ○ What have I failed to do that I said I would do, and how can I make up for it?
  - ○ Who can I contact today, just to keep in touch with them?
  - ○ What can I do to improve an existing process, even if it seems to function properly?
  - ○ How can I identify current processes that are not functioning properly, and what can I do to make the process run effectively?
  - ○ Do my interactions reflect a positive attitude?
  - ○ Can I listen to a complaint without becoming defensive?
  - ○ In what specific ways can I exceed the expectations of someone today?

Based on the answers to these questions, commit to three specific actions over the next week. Then, make ongoing commitments tied to these questions to improve your service orientation. Keep track of your activities, learnings, and progress over the next 90 days.

- **Treat your customers' perceptions as reality because they are reality for them.** Instead of brushing off their concerns, address them seriously. Listen carefully for issues your customers are raising, and show them that you can flex your thinking to take their needs into account. Over the next 60 days, keep track of the instances in which you listen well with customers, including the key information you ascertained and the resolutions you discovered. Learn from instances in which a customers' negative perception is inaccurate, and brainstorm ways to proactively manage the situation before other customers adopt the same view. Make note of your observations and ideas, and share this information with your manager or a coach.

- **Improve your level of service by identifying trends of your customers.** For the next month, write down every customer request, including the administrative tasks as well as the big, strategic requests. At the end of the month, review the tasks and issues you're confronted with, and identify trends. How would you group the types of requests? Which were the most frequent? With these trends in mind, brainstorm ways that you can proactively drive service for your customers. Commit to putting two to three ideas into action over the next few months, and keep track of progress and outcomes.

- **Establish a process for resolving customer issues.** An effective way to handle upset customers is to implement a standard approach to these types of difficult interactions. Research and identify a customer service model to follow such as LAST (Listen, Apologize, Solve, and Thank). Actively listen to gather the information and help diffuse their frustration. (Would you have a similar reaction to the issue at hand?) Apologize if a mistake was made, and if not, find a way to acknowledge their frustration. Solve the issue for the customer and ask if the solution will satisfy their need. Finally, thank the customer for their time and patience.

Over the next two weeks implement a customer service model for handling customer complaints and difficult interactions. Keep track of these interactions. How has this approach impacted your ability to serve your customers? Share your learnings with your manager or a trusted advisor.

- **Set a standard timeframe for resolving customer issues.** For the next 30 to 60 days, set deadlines for gathering information and implementing a solution to every customer issue. Record these dates on your calendar and commit to meeting them. After 30 to 60 days, review your progress.
    - How well did you meet commitments?
    - Where could you have resolved issues quicker?
    - How has this approach impacted your ability to serve your customers?

Take this a step further and create a standard turnaround time for resolving customer issues. This standard should include a timeframe for an initial response (for example, within 24 hours), a schedule for regular follow-up, as well as a timeframe for full resolution.

- **Create standard guidelines for setting up new internal customers.** Create a new customer guide to document how to approach customers with a consistently high service level. Include these tips:
    - When you take on a new customer or group, interview them so you understand their business or role.
    - Ask them: What are your key goals? What changes do you anticipate this year? What are you most looking forward to?
    - Review your team's goals and roles and how you will be serving them.
    - Ask the customers how they see you helping them reach their goals.
    - Take careful notes during the interview.
    - Create a spreadsheet with this information.
    - Update this information regularly as customer needs change and grow.

Review these notes each quarter and note what you need to adjust, delete, or add to make sure you are meeting your customers' needs, while also reaching your own goals. Put this approach into action for all new customers over the next 90 days.

- **When customers express dissenting opinions, try on their point of view without agreeing or disagreeing.** Rather than reject a rigid position, question it and try to determine the principles behind it. Avoid personal clashes by separating the person from the problem, not reacting to negative emotions, and returning to the facts at hand. Be open to hearing the feedback, and let them know that you understand their position. Push yourself to learn or see something that you did not see before the interaction. Try this for 3 to 6 months and keep track of the instances in which you put these approaches into action. Make note of your learnings and the outcomes.

- **Deliberately hone your active listening to uncover customer needs.** You can't excel at serving your customers if you're not truly listening to them. Over the next 30 days, try at least four of the following approaches to develop your active listening skills, and keep track of the results.

  - Pick one or more meetings or discussions each day to deliberately practice active listening. Ask probing questions to uncover needs and check for understanding frequently.

  - Use discussions with friends and family as opportunities to practice listening, influencing, and probing for deeper meaning behind what is said.

  - Remember that listening is a vital component of negotiating and influencing—you need to be "in the moment" to make an impact.

  - Look for opportunities to seek the opinions of colleagues or hiring managers; understand what's important to them and what motivates them.

  - Recognize that not all stakeholders are created equal. Make sure you understand key stakeholders' expectations and requirements. Get coaching to help you designate which stakeholders require "special handling."

After 30 days, reflect on what you found easy and what you found challenging. Make note of your learnings and the outcomes.

- **Read books that provide useful sales and service strategies.** Suggestions include:
  - *Raving Fans: A Revolutionary Approach to Customer Service* by Ken Blanchard and Sheldon Bowles
  - *The Customer Rules: The 39 Essential Rules for Delivering Sensational Service* by Lee Cockerell
  - *High-Tech High-Touch Customer Service: Inspire Timeless Loyalty in the Demanding New World of Social Commerce* by Micah Solomon
  - *All For One: 10 Strategies for Building Trusted Client Partnerships* by Andrew Sobel
  - *The New Gold Standard: 5 Leadership Principles for Creating a Legendary Customer Experience Courtesy of the Ritz-Carlton Hotel Company* by Joseph A Michelli

Dedicate at least 30 minutes a week to reading these resources. For a period of 60 days, make note of the things you learn and new things you would like to try. Review these with your manager or a trusted peer. Discuss how you can incorporate these learnings into your routine.

Ideas for leveraging:
- **Become a mentor to those who seek to improve their customer service.** Offer to guide a few individuals, and meet with them regularly. Review your approach to making and nurturing your partnerships. Observe them during interactions with others, and identify places where they could have taken a better approach. Role-play common customer interactions with them, and help them determine their biggest areas of opportunity.
- **Offer to speak to other departments and groups.** Share your penchant for customer service by being a guest speaker for other teams and within your organization. Present your techniques for uncovering customer needs, resolving issues quickly, soliciting regular feedback, and so on. Share what you have learned of the correlation between how you treat and serve

your direct reports and team, and how they in turn treat and serve their customers. Share real-life stories of victories and defeats, and what you learned from them. Leave time to take questions from the audience.

- **Sponsor a cross-functional customer service think tank.** Work with other leaders to select participants across the organization who demonstrate superior service. Create a charter for the group, and help them set goals. Identify specific problems for them to tackle. Keep track of their work and ideas. Determine a way to share this knowledge across your organization.

- **Create a customer service best practice guide.** List the most common issues that come up when dealing with customers (meeting their needs proactively, gathering regular feedback, and more). Tap into your own experience and knowledge from your peers and network, and present different solutions to resolve or enhance these issues. Publish your guide in the most appropriate way for your organization (via a blog, your internal website, and such).

Behavior 3: Plans and Organizes

Think of someone in your life who you would describe as "extremely organized." What systems does this person implement? How does she plan? People who can effectively plan and organize select and align their work to best support their organization's goals. They can break down work into separate steps and accurately scope out time and resources for each step. They anticipate and prepare for obstacles and establish organizing systems to increase their work efficiency. They can manage many projects and priorities at once, and they store and arrange information (paper and electronic) in a useful and efficient way.

Ideas for improving this skill:

- **Improve your organization skills.** Make sure you have adequate systems in place to make it easier for you to manage your time. During the next 30 days, evaluate how you handle your to-do lists, emails, paperwork, ideas, and such. Take into account how you schedule meetings, follow up on calls and emails, and handle scheduling conflicts. Is the way in which you do these things consistent, effective, and efficient? If not, commit to using a better organization system. Ask peers for their own best practices for organizing work, and look at free, online resources such as Google Apps, Aceproject.com, or Asana. Keep track of what you try and what you like about each until you find a system that works for you. Try it for at least 30 days and then review your "before" and "after" systems and learnings with your manager or an advisor.

- **Evaluate how effective your To-Do list is to ensure you are making progress on your plan.** Often, we concentrate on getting a lot of things done, or "ticking off" items in the order in which they appear on our list. But just because you're crossing off items on your To Do list, it doesn't necessarily mean you're completing the important work—such as tasks that will help you achieve critical goals. Take a different approach by making a master list of tasks and then labeling each item:
  - *Important and urgent* (If not accomplished, there will be negative impact on you.)
  - *Important but not urgent* (It can be done later.)

  Schedule time on your calendar specifically focused on completing each of your #1 priorities. Then, set aside an additional block of time for completing the rest of your tasks—perhaps 30 minutes each day, or a specific amount of time each week or month. Reevaluate your master list as items are added and priorities assigned. Track your progress over a period of 30 days and review your key learnings with your manager or a mentor.

- **Check in with others about expectations before pursuing work.** For the next 60 days, take extra time at the beginning of assignments or projects to understand others' expectations. Ask the other people involved what they'd like to see in the way of deliverables, timing, and what "great" would look like. Ask how they'd approach the task, and if they'd be willing to give you feedback on your work. Push yourself to strive to meet the "great" description. Ask for input and feedback along the way, and keep note of your learnings and outcomes. When the project is complete, compare the outcomes to the expectations. How effective were you at planning your work and meeting (or exceeding) the expectations and timelines? What more could you have done? What did you gain by asking what "great" looks like? Keep track of your work in this area, and share your progress with your manager or a trusted advisor.

- **Plan your work and work your plan.** Try this highly planful approach to each day: Each morning, spend a few minutes mapping out the day's work. Identify what you want to accomplish and when. Build an hour-by-hour schedule for yourself and stick to it; be sure to include time to respond to voicemails and emails. At the end of each day, quickly evaluate your progress. Did you hit your commitments? Did you stick to the schedule? Why? Why not? Do this experiment for one week, and evaluate the results. Track your success with this approach. Later, talk about this information with your manager or a peer.

- **Evaluate how you spend your time to determine if you are working your plan.** For the next week, record all your activities hour by hour on a calendar or in a journal. At the end of the week, look back and evaluate your efforts. When were you the busiest? When were you least productive? What situations/work stimulated action and what slowed you down or led to procrastination? Make note of your learnings and the outcomes. Find at least two things you can do differently to make better use of your time, and commit to implementing them over the following month. Later, share this information with your manager or a trusted friend to help keep you accountable.

- **Create a set of questions to help you break down big projects into manageable pieces.** Begin with:
  - What needs to be accomplished? What is the desired result? When does it need to happen?
  - What are the main tasks or buckets of work that must happen to get this result?
  - What are the specific action steps that make up each of these main tasks?

○ Who will be responsible for each step?

○ How much time will each step take?

Put this checklist into a spreadsheet, a project management program, or in a free (or low-cost) online project management tool such as Aceproject.com or Asana to help you link all the pieces. Commit to using this tool as you plan and manage projects over the next 60 days. Track your progress and review your key learnings with your manager or a trusted advisor.

- **Learn from someone who's great at project management.** Identify someone in your life or work who is known for being a great project manager. Schedule a meeting—or coffee—with that person and ask them questions such as, How do you begin the planning of a new project? What tools do you use to manage projects? How do you go about estimating time for various steps? What communication techniques work best for you? What obstacles do you plan for? What advice would you give someone who struggles in this area? Take notes regarding the conversation. Identify three specific techniques that resonate with you and incorporate them into your approach for 30 days. Keep track of your activities, progress, and learnings in this area and review them monthly with your manager or a friend.

- **Coordinate your planning efforts with other employees, leaders or teams/functions.** Project management requires relying on others to complete work, provide information, review progress, and approve deliverables. Before starting your next project, write down the people who are directly and indirectly involved or affected by this project. Think through whose buy-in or ultimate approval will be required for the project to progress. Think creatively about non-obvious stakeholders. Review your list with a trusted peer. Then, assess how and when each should be involved. Meet or communicate with these stakeholders at appropriate points during each project. Keep notes about their priorities and plans, and incorporate this information into your communications with them. Keep track of your activities, progress, and learnings in this area, and review them monthly with your manager or a friend.

- **Plan ahead for obstacles.** Barriers and obstacles can quickly derail even the best plans. Make planning for obstacles part of your planning process. Some ideas include:

  ○ Consider a wide range of potential issues that may arise. Ask others for their ideas, experiences, and insights to add to this list. Highlight the most likely, and come up with contingency plans for each.

  ○ Ask a trusted peer how you can leverage them better when you encounter a challenge, difficult interpersonal relationship, or roadblock.

  ○ Use technology to help you plan for contingencies. Take advantage of free, online resources such as Google Apps, Aceproject.com, or Asana.

  Choose at least one new idea and implement it for the next 30 days. Track your progress and learnings and review them with your manager or a trusted advisor.

- **Ask for advice on prioritizing and planning your work.** People you complete tasks or assignments for have a unique perspective on what you should be working on, so leverage that. Ask them questions such as, What do you think are my most important responsibilities? Why? What affect does it have when I work on other things? How do you recommend I handle competing priorities? How do you recommend I handle typical distractions like...? Make notes about their comments and recommendations. Identify three specific techniques you can incorporate into your approach. Keep track of your activities, progress, and learnings in this area and review them monthly with your manager or a mentor.

- **Gain additional skills in project management through outside education.** External classes or materials can provide added training and perspective as you hone your project management skills. Consider any of the following:

  ○ Enroll in a course to attain project management certification.

  ○ Attend a workshop on project management processes and tools.

o Subscribe to appropriate journals to stay current on industry trends, state of the art practices, and so on.

Engage fully in the activity and learn as much as you can. Take notes of what is most compelling to you, and act upon your learnings. Commit to doing 2 to 3 concrete things differently afterward for at least 60 days. Monitor your progress, celebrate your successes, and share your experiences regularly with your manager or a trusted advisor.

- **Read books that present useful planning and organizational skills.** Suggestions include:

  o *Simplified Strategic Planning: The No-Nonsense Guide for Busy People Who Want Results Fast* by Robert W. Bradford and Brian Tarcy

  o *Scrum: The Art of Doing Twice the Work in Half the Time* by Jeff Sutherland and JJ Sutherland

  o *The 7 Habits of Highly Effective People* by Stephen R. Covey

  o *The Myth of Multitasking: How "Doing It All" Gets Nothing Done* by Dave Crenshaw

  o *Getting Things Done: The Art of Stress-Free Productivity* by David Allen

Dedicate at least 30 minutes a week to reading these resources. For a period of 60 days, make note of the things you learn and new things you would like to try. Review these with your manager or a trusted peer. Discuss how you can incorporate these learnings into your routine.

Ideas for leveraging:

- **Coach people who want to learn more about how to plan their work.** Offer to spend time reviewing the types of projects they are responsible for and how they approach managing them. Determine what is inefficient or ineffective about their approach. Guide them through the steps of creating a plan, process, and timeline—and planning for obstacles. Encourage them to commit to making two or three changes to their approach. Check in with them afterward to see how they're doing. Give them feedback based on what you observe.

- **Host a virtual or live lunch-n-learn to discuss common organizational or time management problems others face.** Prepare a discussion around the most relevant tips for setting priorities, breaking down a big goal into manageable steps, identifying the resources needed, creating a realistic timeline for each step, and managing problems or roadblocks. Use past examples of successes and failures, and encourage the audience members to do the same. Share tips and advice, and recommend small action steps to help others improve.
- **Conduct one-on-one or small group training sessions about project management.** Topics may include:
  - Defining scope and priorities
  - Leveraging resources
  - Building an integrated project plan
  - Planning for obstacles
  - Tools and templates
- **Take on a new, complex project.** Offer to take a leadership role, or become a member of a project team, where your natural skills are most needed. Over the next 60 days, look for opportunities such as the budgeting process, annual performance reviews, process improvement work, and so on.

Behavior 4: Sets and Drives Priorities

When you have a lot of tasks, how do you decide where to start? If you don't have time to do all the tasks, how do you know which ones are most important? People who set and drive priorities spend time on what's most important. They align the teams they work with and help them see which work has the greatest effect on the end goals. They collaborate and delegate effectively and follow up to ensure the highest-priority work is completed.

Ideas for improving this skill:

- **Understand the challenges and opportunities faced by your organization's leaders.** If possible, get time with one or more leaders in your organization within the next 60 days. Let them know that you want to understand the challenges they experience and the opportunities they see in the organization. Perhaps this can be done over a cup of coffee or a meeting in their office. Ask questions like, "What industry trends represent the greatest opportunity for our organization? What presents the biggest risk to us? Where do you see us as a leader? Where are we lagging? What will be the most important skills and experiences for employees to have in the future? How can my group add more value?" Make note of their answers, prepare to share their point of view with your team, and determine how this new information affects your group's priorities. Consider inviting them to speak to your team. In addition, commit to at least two things you'll do differently as a result of what you've learned. Share your learnings and action plan with a trusted advisor.

- **When working on a team, review your team's priorities to determine how closely it is aligned with the end goals of the organization.** Over the next 30 days, schedule time to ask yourself these questions:
  - What are we trying to accomplish?
  - What have we accomplished?
  - Does everyone have a clear goal?
  - Does everyone understand our norms and ways of working?
  - Where are we headed as a team? What does success look like?
  - What are the biggest challenges we face?

  Take time to build a comprehensive plan for closing the gaps between the current state and the desired state. Work with your team to review and implement it. Keep track of your work in this area, and what progress you make.

- **Evaluate how effective your To-Do list is in terms of focusing on your priorities.** Often, we concentrate on getting a lot of things done or "ticking off" items in the order in which they appear on our list. But just because you're crossing off items on your To Do list, it doesn't necessarily mean you're completing the important work—meaning tasks that can help you achieve critical goals. Take a different approach by making a master list of tasks and then labeling each item:

○ *Important and urgent* (If not accomplished, there will be negative impact on you.)

○ *Important but not urgent* (It can be done later.)

○ All other

Schedule time on your calendar specifically focused on completing each of your #1 priorities. Then, set aside an additional block of time for completing the rest of your tasks—perhaps 30 minutes each day or a specific amount of time each week or month. Reevaluate your master list as items are added and priorities assigned. Track your progress over a period of 30 days and review your key learnings with your manager or a trusted mentor.

• **Keep track of how you spend your time each day to assess if it aligns with your priorities.** Throughout the day, assess how you're spending your time. At first, make note of things that you spend an hour or more on each day. As you get in the habit of doing this, concentrate on smaller blocks of time. Then, list activities that tie you up intermittently but which are hard to assign times to (for example, checking Facebook and personal emails) and assign a rough estimate of time to them.

After a few days, look back and assess which tasks were the best use of your time. What goals did you accomplish and how important are they? What did you fail to work on or complete? What are your main distractors or time wasters? What times of the day are you most energized and productive? How often should you take a physical break—even for just a few minutes—to get re-energized? Commit to making at least two changes to the way in which you manage your time during the day. Track your progress over a period of 30 days and review your key learnings with your manager or a friend.

• **Ask yourself key questions about how you prioritize your work.** Begin with:

○ What work regularly needs to be accomplished?

○ What are the best results I could possibly achieve?

- What are the main tasks or buckets of work that must happen to achieve these results?
- What are the most important tasks?
- What types of issues emerge that distract me from focusing on the more important tasks?
- What other things or habits—that I bring on myself—cause me to be distracted?
- How can I manage these issues differently, so I can focus on the critical few tasks?

Review this information with your manager or a trusted peer. Ask for feedback. Discuss what distracts you from doing your most important work. Brainstorm solutions. Identify two to four concrete things you can do to change your approach. Track your progress over a period of 30 days and review your key learnings with your manager or a peer.

- **Learn from someone who's great at prioritizing.** Identify someone who is strong in this area. Schedule a meeting—or coffee—with that person and ask questions such as, How do you prioritize your work? How do you manage competing priorities? How do you determine whether something is truly urgent—or whether others are just demanding something to be done? What tools do you use to prioritize your work? What obstacles affect your ability to prioritize? What advice would you give someone who struggles in this area? Take notes regarding the conversation. Identify three specific techniques that resonate with you and incorporate them into your approach. Keep track of your activities, progress, and learnings in this area and review them monthly with your manager or an advisor.

- **Do a big-picture review of your projects and reconfirm priorities.** Within the next 30 days, set aside several hours to review every major project or ongoing responsibility you have. After everything is laid out, review how much of it should be labeled important and urgent. Do this by assigning a level of "urgency" and "impact" using a 4-point scale (1 = low, 4 = high). Those with 4 points will be high in urgency or impact or both. Following are some questions to help you determine urgency and impact:

- Does this project have a direct impact on completing my goals?
- Who wants or needs this project to be completed?
- What would happen if this project weren't completed within the requested timeframe?
- What would happen if this project weren't completed at all?

If too many projects are deemed urgent, talk with a friend or advisor about how to prioritize them. Ask for ideas for how to shift resources toward the highest priority work. After you try this once, keep track of the results of this prioritization—specifically, what worked and what didn't. Note your learnings and adjust your approach the next time.

- **Gather feedback from those around you about your prioritization skills.** Prepare a brief survey asking those around you to give you their honest feedback about your skills. Find a way to ensure that the results are anonymous so that people will feel comfortable being candid. (Try a free web-survey tool such as Survey Monkey or by asking a neutral third party to compile the results.) Limit the survey to just a few relevant questions, such as

  - How well do I prioritize goals and tasks? (4-point scale, 1 being "very well" and 4 being "not at all well")
  - Overall, would you describe me as a person who strategically prioritizes tasks? (4-point scale, 1 being "yes, absolutely and consistently" and 4 being "no, not at all, never")
  - If you would not describe me as someone who prioritizes strategically, please explain what I could do differently to improve my skills in this area. (Open-ended question)

After you review the results, make a point to thank your friends, family, or co-workers for their participation. Give them a brief summary of what you learned about yourself. Then choose the top two issues that your team identified and devise a plan to address them. Keep track of your activities and learnings, and share them with your manager or a mentor on a monthly basis.

- **Read books about setting priorities and strategies for driving shared organizational goals/pursuits.** Suggestions include:
  - *Getting Organized at Work: 24 Lessons to Set Goals, Establish Priorities, and Manage Your Time* by Kenneth Zeigler
  - *The Power of Alignment: How Great Companies Stay Centered and Accomplish Extraordinary Things* by George Labovitz and Victor Rosansky
  - *The Accountability Revolution: Achieve Breakthrough Results in Half the Time* by Mark Samuel
  - *The Great Workplace: How to Build It, How to Keep It, and Why It Matters* by Michael Burchell and Jennifer Robbin
  - *The Advantage: Why Organizational Health Trumps Everything Else In Business* by Patrick M. Lencioni

  Dedicate at least 30 minutes a week to reading these resources. For a period of 60 days, make note of the things you learn and new things you would like to try. Review these with your manager or a trusted peer. Discuss how you can incorporate these learnings into your routine.

Ideas for leveraging:

- **Coach people who seek to improve their prioritization skills.** Offer to spend time reviewing the work they are responsible for and how they approach prioritizing it. Determine how they make decisions and how they spend their time. Guide them through the steps of prioritizing work and planning for distractions. Encourage them to commit to making two or three changes to their approach based on your advice and feedback. Check in with them afterward to see how they're doing, and give them feedback based on what you observe.

- **Host a virtual or live lunch-n-learn to discuss setting strong priorities.** Create a brief overview of your approach for prioritizing work. Include examples of a typical day or project, your approach to prioritizing work, how you handle competing priorities and how you manage distractions. Talk about lessons learned, obstacles encountered, and your approach to managing unexpected events. Share tips and advice, and recommend small action steps to help others improve.

- **Develop a short presentation teaching others how to improve their prioritization skills.** Create a presentation that walks others through your methods to:
  - Identify the highest priority work.
  - Manage competing priorities.
  - Manage time-consuming peer or client requests—and other distractors.
  - Identify resources to help you prioritize.
  - Create a realistic timeline for priorities.
  - Translate priorities into weekly and daily to-do lists.
- **Host a virtual or in-person training session with people who want to improve in this area.** As an alternative, share your presentation online: Shoot a short video and post it on YouTube, or create a PowerPoint presentation and post it on your own blog, or on another platform.
- **Get involved in a new, challenging project.** Offer to take a leadership role or become a member of a project team where your natural skills in prioritization could help. Look for opportunities to help prioritize work related to budgeting, annual performance reviews, process improvement work, and more.

Behavior 5: Overcomes Obstacles

Think of people you know who are resilient and resourceful. What tools or approaches do they use? People who overcome obstacles get the job done despite obstacles in process, people, or business. They can maneuver through challenges with skill and confidence. They have a sense of urgency: They're willing to adapt when needed and shifts gears comfortably. They are skilled at negotiating with others to secure the resources needed to meet their commitments. They call upon connections as needed to resolve issues.

Ideas for improving this skill:

- **Improve the way in which you handle obstacles or challenges.** Some ideas include:
  - Plan ahead for obstacles. Consider a wide range of potential issues that may arise. Ask others for their ideas, experiences, and insights to add to this list. Highlight the most likely, and come up with contingency plans for each.
  - Ask a trusted peer how you can leverage obstacles better when you encounter a challenge, difficult interpersonal relationship, or roadblock.
  - Use technology to help you plan for contingencies. Take advantage of free, online resources such as Google Apps or aceprojects.com.

  Choose at least one new idea and implement it for the next 30 days. Track your progress and learnings and review them with your manager or an advisor.

- **Expect the unexpected and prepare.** Over the next 30 days, consider an assignment or project you're starting, and brainstorm alternative approaches to it, given different unexpected constraints. For example, brainstorm ways that you would modify your approach in a scenario in which you had fewer participants than expected. Or less money. Or a tighter deadline. Or broader scope. Thinking of options can help you be prepared if you have to shift gears in short order. Share your thoughts on this process, and your alternative approaches, with a mentor, and discuss other situations when multiple options are frequently needed.

- **Build a broader network to influence outcomes more effectively.** Building a broad network of relationships can be useful in helping you overcome obstacles. For example, when you face a situation in which significant setbacks appear or where you must quickly change directions, leverage your network to gain information and insights, knowledge, and support. Over the next 60 days, consider taking a disciplined approach to networking—consciously developing contacts in a variety of industries or areas. Leverage your current network to make connections with new people you don't yet know. After the connection has been made, use your mutual connection to build common ground and establish trust. Offer to do the same for others. Keep track of your new connections. At the same time, nurture your current network by sending a note of greeting to keep them close. Share your network plan with a trusted friend and ask for feedback and whether he can suggest any of his contacts for you to meet.

- **Determine what slows you down in the face of obstacles.** When you're faced with a roadblock, what makes you hesitate— or undermines your ability—to resolve it? With what type of difficulties do you find yourself feeling reluctant to move forward or feel your resolve wane? Over the next few weeks, keep track of specific obstacles that are presented to you. Note the problem, who surfaced the problem, what action you take, and the ultimate outcome. Spend some time assessing, in each case, what slowed you down or created an obstacle. Look for patterns: Are you avoiding certain subjects? Do specific people make you uncomfortable? Is there a certain type of work you dislike? Did you have the data you need? What personal habits, such as procrastination, being disorganized, or uncertainty about the best approach, impeded your ability to solve problems? After you identify the sources of your hesitation, you can more effectively address them. Review your notes with a trusted peer or mentor. Over the next 60 days, commit to taking concrete actions to stop avoiding or hesitating to dig in and get things done. Keep track of your work in this area, and share your learnings with your manager or your mentor.

- **Build your confidence.** Sometimes, it can be intimidating to take high-profile steps needed to resolve obstacles. To become more assertive and sure of yourself, try one or all of these techniques:
  - Find a coach or role model who can help you learn to be more assertive.
  - Study how assertive people start discussions, deal with interruptions, express their views, and respond to criticism.

o Practice clearly stating your point of view directly and confidently, especially when you're in safe environments, interacting with those close to you. Keep a journal of when you try this (both within and outside of work) and review this with a friend or a mentor to demonstrate your progress.

o Pay attention to how you feel when you ask for what you want. Note the difference in how other people treat you when you are assertive.

Use these reflections to motivate you to continue to assert yourself. Share your learnings with your manager or a friend.

- **Learn to say no.** When you're focused and directing your time and resources toward the right things, you'll have to turn down less important work. If this makes you uncomfortable, practice saying "no" when necessary over the next 60 days. Some tips to keep in mind:

o This is professional, not personal.

o Be polite, yet firm when you decline to participate.

o Offer an alternative if possible (an idea for another resource or a better time/date when you may be able to help). Use language such as "I may not be able to do _____ by _____, but this is what I can do: _____."

o If you have to say "no," do not procrastinate letting the person know.

Keep track of your progress in this area, and share your results with your manager or an advisor.

- **Develop your negotiation skills.** Chances are you'll need to obtain additional resources that are in high demand or may be controlled by other people. You'll need strong negotiation and influencing skills to do this effectively. Over the next 60 days, work on your negotiation skills. Observe others who are master negotiators, and take note of what techniques they use. Take one of them to coffee and pick her brain about her tried-and-true negotiation tips. How does she change her communication style to be more persuasive? How does she "trade" to get what she needs? Commit to practicing at least three new techniques, and share your progress with your manager or a mentor.

- **Turn to your network to dig for resources.** When the skills and budget you need for a project are just not available to you, determine how and where to find these resources. Who has the necessary expertise? What could you potentially "trade" for access to these people? What are the steps required to request additional funds? What other work could be eliminated (or put on hold) to make resources available? Who in your network can you turn to for help connecting to resources? Discuss your findings with your manager or a trusted advisor.

- **Develop an Issues Resolution system to keep you on track.** Find a simple, yet effective way to organize and track all open, unresolved, and recurring issues. It can also prevent key items from falling "through the cracks." Keeping them front and center will ensure that even the smallest issues are dealt with. This may be a chart on your wall, a spreadsheet, or a file system. Whatever method you choose, commit to creating and implementing it within the next 30 days. Show your manager or a mentor and peers your system and ask for their feedback. Make notes about how this system increases your ability to get your job done.

- **Get involved with the launch of a new product or service.** Learn about being adaptable from a real-life example. Within the next 30 days, identify a new product or service at an organization you know, and ask to sit in on meetings and pay attention to the ways that the team anticipates and prepares for the change ahead. Observe how they anticipate and manage potential pushback, identify stakeholder concerns, build the business case for change, and develop/pursue communication processes. Make notes of the themes and concepts that resonate the most with you, and keep a list of the things/ideas that can help you be more adaptable and results-oriented in your own projects. Share your learnings with your manager or a friend.

- **Learn from past patterns.** By learning from the experiences of others, we can better predict, or at least prepare, for shifts that might occur. Over the next 60 days, poll each of your trusted friends or co-workers to learn about their experiences when work efforts, presentations, or projects have had to shift course quickly. For the examples that they provide, list the cause and the response. Look for patterns. Is the shift typically due to changing business conditions? A new stakeholder on the scene? A customer trend? How did your colleagues respond to these shifts? What was successful? What did they learn? Would they have done anything different in retrospect? Review your analysis with a trusted peer, and talk about how you might apply your learnings right away.

- **Learn from those who are known for smoothly overcoming obstacles.** Identify someone you interact with who resolves issues with ease and skill. Talk to him about how he reaches solutions to roadblocks. Ask if he has a certain decision-making process he follows, what kinds of data or information he relies on, and from whom he seeks input. Ask what mistakes he has made and how those impacted future judgments. Make note of his suggestions and ideas, and commit to trying at least two of them over the next 30 days.

- **Read books that detail strategies for overcoming various types of obstacles.** Suggestions include:
  - *Making Ideas Happen: Overcoming the Obstacles Between Vision and Reality* by Scott Belsky
  - *Tapping into Ultimate Success: How to Overcome Any Obstacle and Skyrocket Your Results* by Jack Canfield and Pamela Bruner
  - *Why People Fail: The 16 Obstacles to Success and How You Can Overcome Them* by Simon Reynolds
  - *Adaptability: The Art of Winning in an Age of Uncertainty* by Max McKeown
  - *The Power of Persistence: Real Life Stories of Real People Creating Extraordinary Results* by Justin Sachs

  Dedicate at least 30 minutes a week to reading these resources. For a period of 60 days, make note of the things you learn and new things you would like to try. Review these with your manager or a trusted peer. Discuss how you can incorporate these learnings into your routine.

Ideas for leveraging:

- **Coach people who seek to improve their ability to overcome obstacles.** Offer to spend time reviewing the types of projects they are responsible for and the most common obstacles they encounter. Determine what they do that is inefficient or ineffective, and share your own techniques when planning for obstacles—and "getting back on the horse" when something goes wrong. Identify and together discuss occasions in which they could have been more adaptable in the past, and perhaps how you've tackled similar problems in your experience. Encourage them to commit to making two or three changes to their approach. Check in with them afterward to see how they're doing. Give them feedback based on what you observe.

- **Host a virtual or live lunch-n-learn to discuss common obstacles and roadblocks.** Prepare a discussion around the most relevant tips for managing problems or roadblocks (such as lack of funding, difficult personalities, and changes in scope). Use past examples of successes and failures and encourage the audience members to do the same. Share tips and advice, and recommend small action steps to help others improve. Keep track of the work you do and the impact it seems to have on others.

- **Develop a short presentation reviewing your approach to achieving desired results in spite of obstacles that arise.** Include tips, best practices, resources, and real-world examples or cases to showcase your experience and knowledge. Host a virtual or in-person training session with people who want to improve in this area. As an alternative, share your presentation online: Shoot a short video and post it on YouTube, or create a PowerPoint presentation and post it on your own blog, or on another platform.

- **Conduct one-on-one or small group training sessions about different topics in overcoming obstacles, such as the following:**
  - Staying the course while remaining adaptable
  - Negotiating for what you need

- Influencing others
- Thinking creatively about resources
- Leveraging your people
- Examples of tenacity in action
- Leveraging tools and processes
- Creating a "Plan B"

Behavior 6: Demonstrates Technological Savvy

Our world moves faster all the time with the constant development of new technologies. How businesses leverage technology can often determine their level of success. People who demonstrate technological savvy are quick and confident adopters of new technologies. They make it a priority to seek out and learn the latest advancements in technology and tools to drive the business forward.

Ideas for improving this skill:

- **Find someone in a job or role you are interested in, who successfully leverages technology.** Ask this person specific questions about how she uses technology, such as, What tools do you find the most invaluable for your job? What sites do you leverage to gather new ideas? What efficiency tools or websites do you use? What software do you use every day? Make notes about these tools and techniques, and commit to trying two to three during the next 90 days. During this time, record your questions or concerns and follow up with your mentor regularly. Reflect periodically on your progress in this area, and discuss your learnings with your manager or a friend.

- **Spend time learning about data analysis tools and how to use them.** Start with programs such as Microsoft Excel or SAS and take the tutorials to learn how this tool can help you make decisions. Practice the techniques you learn with small decisions. As you build comfort, allow these types of tools to take a bigger role in your data analysis and decision-making process. Put this approach into action for the next 60 days. Make note of your learnings and the outcomes. Later, share this information with your manager or an advisor.

- **Learn how to leverage social media to help an organization.** Explore various uses of sites such as LinkedIn, Facebook (pages), Twitter, and pick a favorite organization. How does this organization use these tools to reach customers or improve processes? Watch or research how others (including that organization's competitors and customers) use these tools as well. Keep track of what you learn for the next 30 days, and share your learnings with your manager or a peer.

- **Scan job listings at top companies to identify skills in demand.** Take special interest in the technological requirements and expectations associated with positions you would like to have. Use this as a jumping ground to explore new tools and techniques that you may not employ currently. Push yourself to learn at least one of these new technologies in the next 60 days. Track your efforts in this area, and share your learnings with your mentor.

- **Expose yourself to new technology by observing those in leadership and administrative roles as they use their systems throughout the day.** Ask them which tools they rely on most, and how they increase their productivity. This will ensure you have a solid foundation of administrative technical savvy, as well as knowledge of the tools necessary to advance in your desired field. Commit to learning these tools over the next 60 days, and keep track of your training and progress. Review what you've learned, and how you've applied it, with a trusted advisor at the end of the 60 days.

- **Explore and determine how you can use technology to improve customer service.** Research and identify existing and new technology in use in your desired industry to improve the customer experience. Examples could include websites, voicemail, email, and software. Evaluate how each improves, or potentially could improve, an organization's capability to respond to customers, to communicate with customers, to increase marketing channels, to manage the customer relationship, to analyze data (such as purchasing patterns and preferences), or to facilitate self-service options for customers. Take 60 days to learn about these technologies and discuss your findings with a friend.

- **Read books that encourage technology in a work environment.** Suggestions include the following:
  - *The Digital Workplace: How Technology is Liberating Work* by Paul Miller
  - *Aligning Technology with Strategy* by *Harvard Business Review*
  - *Groundswell: Winning in a World Transformed by Social Technologies* by Charlene Li and Josh Bernoff
  - *The New Technology Elite: How Great Companies Optimize Both Technology Consumption and Production* by Vinnie Mirchandani

  Dedicate at least 30 minutes a week to reading these resources. For a period of 30 days, make note of the things you learn and new things you would like to try. Review these with a trusted peer. Discuss how you can incorporate these learnings into your routine.

Ideas for leveraging:

- **Conduct one-on-one or small group training sessions about different topics related to technology.** Examples include:
  - Leveraging data analysis tools
  - Using social media
  - Overcoming fear of technology
  - "Tool of the month"—exploring a new technology each month.

  Select tools and programs that you feel passionate about. Encourage two-way communication. Make it relevant by asking the attendees for examples and questions. Keep track of the work you do and the impact it seems to have on others.

- **Develop a short presentation about getting the most out of technology.** Include tips, best practices, resources, and real-world examples and cases to showcase your experience and knowledge of tools that are most relevant to your job. Host a virtual or in-person training session with people who want to improve in this area. As an alternative, share your presentation online: Shoot a short video and post it on YouTube, or create a PowerPoint presentation and post it on your own blog, or on another platform. Keep track of your work in this area and share your learnings with an advisor.

- **Coach someone who needs to develop their technology skills.** Help them determine their specific areas to improve, and discuss what hinders them from doing more in this area. Talk about starting slow and learning one step at a time. Share concrete suggestions for how to become more familiar with technology. If appropriate, have them observe you for a period of time. Meet with them regularly to review their progress.

- **Offer to lend your technical skills to a project team.** Help a cross-functional team or a special task force responsible for driving important results. Offer to lead its technology efforts, and apply your expertise to its efforts. Keep track of the work you do and the impact it seems to have on others.

- **Learn about a technology used in a field or industry different than your own.** Take the initiative to familiarize yourself with a technology used in another field, perhaps in an area that has always interested you. Leverage your network or connections to identify someone you can interview in the chosen position or field, or set up a visit to a specific location if more appropriate. Ask a lot of questions. Strive, as you learn about the new technology, to apply that other field's knowledge to a current area in your own organization or job; see if you generate any new perspectives, applications, or ideas.

5

Competency: Communicates Effectively

Behavior 1: Writes Effectively

Behavior 2: Tailors Interpersonal Approach

Behavior 3: Shares Information

Behavior 4: Develops and Delivers Compelling Presentations

Behavior 5: Collaborates Across Boundaries

Behavior 6: Adopts a Cross-Cultural Mindset

Overview of Competency

The ability to communicate effectively, in different settings and with everyone we encounter, affects nearly everything we do and can accomplish. Research shows that the ability to communicate well is hampered by long-term use of electronics, yet it's seen as the single most important indicator of success in the workplace. Because there are many facets to communication, there are many areas to strive to master.

Behavior 1: Writes Effectively

A great writer can write clearly and succinctly across a variety of different communication mediums, such as articles, presentations, and emails. Great writers can break down complex information into bite-sized, readable messages. They write in an engaging and conversational way, use proper grammar, and demonstrate good email and texting etiquette.

Ideas for improving this skill:

- **Focus on writing better emails.** Writing an effective email is a specific kind of writing skill. It can be tricky to write messages that are not too short (missing key information) or too long (including extraneous information). If you struggle to create effective email messages, focus on reading books and articles that offer guidance. Suggestions include *E-Mail: A Write It Well Guide* by Janis Fisher Chan.

  Commit to reading at least one email improvement article per week, for the next 4 weeks. Apply what you learn immediately, and note if you receive different reactions or feedback than before. Keep track of your actions and learnings and discuss your progress with your manager or a mentor.

- **Be clear about your purpose in writing.** Take a moment upfront to specifically decide on the purpose of your written communication. Is it to inform? Is it to request a certain action? Is it to schedule a meeting? To convince your readers to do something (or to stop doing something)? Consider what you want to accomplish and the impression you want to convey. For the next 60 days, consider these questions before you begin writing your communication. Write your purpose and the results you want on Post-it® Notes and place them on your computer screen as you write. These visual reminders can help you write a presentation that stays on track with your goals. Note how this approach affects the effectiveness of your writing, and share the results with your manager or a trusted friend.

- **Find a writing coach.** Within the next 30 days, choose a peer or leader who writes clear, understandable emails and other business communications. Ask this person to be your writing coach to share tips about grammar and spelling, to explain how to format an email for best response, and to review and edit your past communications. Going forward, have this person review your emails or presentations before you finalize them. Ask for specific feedback and make edits based on the advice. Share what you learn with your manager or a mentor.

- **Know your audience.** Before beginning to write an email, presentation or memo, take time to analyze whom you are writing to. Make yourself an audience analysis checklist that includes these questions:

o What does my audience already know about my subject?

o Does it have an opinion about it?

o Is there history that I should take into account?

o Will my communication affect anything else in its world? How or why?

The answers to these questions will inform how you create your message. For example, if you know your audience will be opposed to your information, you'll need to be empathetic yet persuasive. If your audience will see your message as just more work for it, you'll need to clearly spell out the benefits of the work. Use your audience analysis checklist for the next 30 days. Note how it helps you prepare your messaging. Share your progress and insights with your manager or a friend.

• **Sharpen your proofreading skills.** Seemingly minor typos and grammatical errors can have a negative impact on how your messages are received. Try these proofreading techniques to catch your mistakes before you share them with the world:

o Print out important emails before you send them. It's much easier to proofread your message when it's not on the screen in front of you.

o Read your message backward, one sentence at a time. Typos and misspellings will jump out at you if you start from the end of your piece.

o Read with a partner. Ask someone to scan your message as you read it out loud.

o Take a break. After you've written an important memo, report, or message, set it aside for at least several hours, if not overnight. It will be much easier to see your mistakes with fresh eyes.

Commit to trying these techniques over the next 30 days. Notice if your writing improves as a result. Share your insights and progress with your manager or a peer.

- **Read books that provide guidance for writing well in the workplace.** Suggestions include:
  - *The Truth About the New Rules of Business Writing* by Natalie Canavor and Claire Meirowitz
  - *Writing That Works; How to Communicate Effectively in Business* by Kenneth Roman and Joel Raphaelson
  - *The Executive Guide to E-mail Correspondence: Including Model Letters for Every Situation* by Dawn-Michelle Baude
  - *Write Up the Corporate Ladder: Successful Writers Reveal the Techniques That Help You Write with Ease and Get Ahead* by Kevin Ryan

  Dedicate at least 30 minutes a week to reading these resources. For a period of 60 days, make note of the things you learn and new things you would like to try. Review these with your manager or a trusted peer. Discuss how you can incorporate these learnings into your routine.

Ideas for leveraging:

- **Coach people who need help with their writing skills.** Review your approach to planning for different types of communication. Share with them the top five resources you use (blogs, websites, books, and more) to help with your own writing. Review their business communications before they finalize them, and share your feedback (and logic) with them. Identify places where they could have been clearer and more succinct.

  Meet with them over a period of several weeks. Assess how effectively you coach, and share your activities and learnings with your manager or a peer.

- **Develop a short presentation about business writing fundamentals.** Include tips, best practices, resources, and real-world examples and cases to showcase your experience and knowledge. Topics may include:
  - Organizing your thoughts
  - Self-editing
  - Proofreading

○ Deciding what to cover in the first paragraph of a paper or memo

Host a virtual or in-person training session with people who want to become better writers. As an alternative, share your presentation online: Shoot a short video and post it on YouTube, or create a PowerPoint presentation and post it on your own blog, or on another platform. Keep track of your work in this area and share your learnings with your manager or a friend.

- **Host a virtual or live lunch-n-learn to discuss email etiquette.** Prepare a discussion about creating effective and courteous business emails. Discuss common problems that people face, such as poor subject lines or who and when to "cc" or "bcc" others on emails. Share past examples of successes and failures and encourage others to do the same. Share tips and advice and recommend small action steps to help others practice and improve. Keep track of the work you do and the impact it seems to have on others.

- **Offer to be someone's editor.** Help others improve their writing skills by offering to edit their important memos, emails and presentations. Take the time to review your edits with them, explaining the logic behind your comments. Show them different ways of phrasing ideas and better approaches to organizing their thoughts. Keep track of the work you do, and the impact you feel it's having on others.

Behavior 2: Tailors Interpersonal Approach

Different skills are required to interact successfully with many different kinds of people. The ability to tailor our interpersonal approach makes us come across as warm and approachable. People who tailor their approaches know when and how to adapt their communication style for different types of people. They listen patiently to understand and are good at reading others' reactions. They show empathy for others' experiences.

Ideas for improving this skill:

- **Improve your listening skills.** If you suspect that you may not be a good listener, ask yourself these questions, and make note of the answers:

  - Do you interrupt others frequently?

  - Do you show impatience, either verbally or through your body language?

  - Do you suggest solutions before a problem is fully explained?

  - Do you spend more time talking than listening?

  - Do you often find your mind wandering and miss what was said?

  - Do you find yourself thinking about your response while someone else is talking to you?

  - Do you divide your attention between others and things like checking your phone?

  If the answer to two or more is "yes," then select two concrete things that you will begin doing differently immediately. Some ideas to try follow:

  - Deliberately practice active listening during a meeting. Remove distractions, ask clarifying and open-ended questions, listen intently, and don't interrupt or make assumptions. Ask probing questions to uncover needs and check for understanding frequently. Later, make note of what seemed to work well about this conversation.

  - Use discussions with friends and family as opportunities to practice listening, influencing, and probing for deeper meaning behind what is said. Later, ask for feedback and track which techniques seemed to be more effective than others.

  - Look for opportunities to seek the opinions of colleagues; understand what's important to them and what motivates them.

  Keep track of your actions and learnings over a 30-day period, noting what was easiest and most challenging for you. Discuss your progress with your manager or a trusted mentor.

- **Increase two-way communication with those around you.**
Build opportunities to gather others' input to improve your
ability to understand them. Some ideas include:

  - Ask for comments and questions (along with the best means
  of providing this feedback) at the end of email messages.

  - Allow time at the end of meeting agendas (face-to-face or
  virtual) to answer questions and listen to concerns.

  - Solicit opinions and feedback from others via monthly phone
  calls or email messages.

  - Schedule a "gathering feedback" step at regular intervals
  during complicated, multifaceted projects.

  For the next 30 days, try different methods of soliciting feedback to see which feel most comfortable to you. Keep track of
  your efforts and review your progress with your manager or a
  trusted peer.

- **Learn from a leader who has great interpersonal skills.**
Identify someone who you believe communicates well with
many different types of people. Over the next 30 days, observe
this person in a variety of settings: small group meetings, one-
on-one sessions, and large presentations. Note how she tailors
her approach based on different personalities, moods, and
organization levels. Keep a list of techniques that you will try
yourself going forward and then implement them. Note how
people react to you as you alter your own style to better match
theirs. Share your learnings and insights with your manager or
a friend.

- **Know your audience.** Prepare yourself before high-profile
conversations, whether they are with a group or an individual.
Make yourself an audience analysis checklist that includes these
questions:

  - What does my audience already know about my subject?

  - Does it have an opinion about it already?

  - Is there history there that I should take into account?

  - Will my communication affect anything else in its world?
  How or why?

The answers to these questions can help you plan your approach, such as your tone of voice, level of detail to share, and how to use humor (or not), and will allow you to anticipate their questions. Use your audience analysis checklist for the next 30 days. Note how it helps you tailor your messages and style to particular audiences. Share your successes and insights with your manager or an advisor.

- **Practice "conflict conscious" communication to engage others during difficult conversations.** Try one or more of these approaches over 30 days and keep track of your efforts and results:

  - Practice *active listening* to diffuse conflict and gather information. Check for understanding by restating their point, ask follow-up questions, and use nonverbal cues to demonstrate that you understand what is being said (such as nodding head, taking notes, and making eye contact).

  - Before responding to someone, ask yourself questions such as, Do I understand their position? Are they making any assumptions that I can clarify? What would I do if I were in their position? Can I argue their position if I had to? Once you understand their position, formulate a response that demonstrates your complete understanding of the issue.

  - Refrain from making negative statements during conflict by focusing on facts. Avoid attacks, assumptions, and empty or throwaway statements.

  - Do not reject dissenting opinions. Instead, try on their point of view without agreeing or disagreeing. Question their stance and try to determine the principles behind it.

  - Stay calm during interactions. When possible, use words to explain your point of view rather than emotion. Staying calm will encourage others to calm down and match your tone, resulting in a more productive exchange.

  - When you stand up to others, begin by assuming they mean well and acknowledge their good intentions: (that is, "I appreciate that you want the project to be successful. I have another way to look at what we need to do.") This method allows you to get your point across without overriding or disrespecting the other person's opinion.

Make note of which approaches you commit to trying and for a period of 30 days, keep track of your efforts and learnings. Later, reflect on themes in results—what you found easy and what you found challenging. Make note of your learnings and the outcomes. Later, share this information with your manager or a friend.

- **Record, remember, and recall information about people.** When meeting people for the first time, repeat their name at least three times in the conversation to help ensure that you remember it. During your conversation ask them about something unique to them, such as where they grew up, what their interests are, who they cheered for in the Super Bowl, and so on. When you get back to your office, put the information you've gathered in your contacts. The next time you see them, recall the information from the last conversation and build on the conversation.

- **Give people your full attention.** Commit to staying completely attuned when others are sharing information with you. Close your computer and put your phone down during these interactions. Look people in the eye, nod to show understanding, and try to reframe and repeat the messages you hear.

- **Ask people how they are doing.** Ask questions like: "How's it going? Is everything all right?" Look them in the eye, wait for their response, and then acknowledge it. Work on improving not only general questioning but also specific work project questions, such as "How are you feeling about the report results?" When possible, offer a suggestion and your assistance to help them out. Record what you learn about each individual and how you responded.

Keep track of which techniques worked best for you in engaging and learning about others. Share your learnings with your manager or a peer.

- **Address an array of viewpoints.** Being prepared to address multiple viewpoints can help you adapt your communications approach on-the-fly, according to the group or individual.

Within the next 30 days, think about a project you're working on that affects different individuals or groups of people, and jot down how each individual or group might respond to the project approach or direction. Then ask yourself these questions: What would you have to say to stakeholders to help them understand the benefits? How do the messages vary? How can you build a solid case to convince each stakeholder? Discuss your varying messages with your manager or a mentor, and talk about where to apply this analysis in upcoming work.

- **Learn to read and handle others' reactions.** Often people won't come out and say how they actually feel about something you've said or an idea you've suggested. To build your skills around reading actual (unstated) reactions, try these techniques:

  - *Watch body language.* If people have their arms crossed, or won't look you in the eye, or become flushed, they may be having a negative reaction. In this case, you can clarify in the moment, or wait a while before following up.

  - *Ask specific questions.* If people seem confused or give you a vague response, ask them questions such as "Do you understand what I'm saying?" or "Do you have any follow-up questions?"

  - *Summarize what you think they may be feeling.* In a non-confrontational tone, do your best to state what they may be feeling: "It looks like you might be confused about this plan" or "I think you might not agree with me here." This will at least give people words to react to, so you can get to what they are truly feeling.

  Commit to trying these techniques over the next 30 days, and note how they work for you. Share your insights and progress with your manager or an advisor.

- **Read books that provide useful tips on interpersonal acuity and/or emotional intelligence.** Suggestions include:

  - *Communicating Effectively* by *Harvard Business Review*

  - *Power Listening: Mastering the Most Critical Business Skill of All* by Bernard T. Ferrari

○ *Emotional Intelligence: A Practical Guide to Making Friends with Your Emotions and Raising Your EQ* by Ian Tuhovsky

Dedicate at least 30 minutes a week to reading these resources. For a period of 60 days, make note of the things you learn and new things you would like to try. Review these with your manager or a trusted peer. Discuss how you can incorporate these learnings into your routine.

Ideas for leveraging:

- **Coach people who need help with their interpersonal communication skills.** Review your approach to communicating with different types of people. Share with them your own tips for reacting on-the-fly and handling different reactions. Watch them in different types of interactions, and identify places where they could have been clearer, more empathetic, and so on. Meet with them over a period of several weeks.

- **Develop a short presentation about interpersonal communication.** Include tips, best practices, resources, and real-world examples and cases to showcase your experience and knowledge. Topics may include:

  ○ Reading people

  ○ Diffusing conflict

  ○ Varying your tone of voice for impact

  Host a virtual or in-person training session with people who want to become better presenters. As an alternative, share your presentation online: Shoot a short video and post it on YouTube, or create a PowerPoint presentation and post it on your own blog, or on another platform. Keep track of your work in this area and share your learnings with a friend.

- **Host a virtual or live lunch-n-learn to discuss interpersonal communication.** Prepare a discussion around communicating effectively with all kinds of people. Discuss common problems that people face, such as not listening effectively or being inflexible in their approach. Share past examples of successes and failures and encourage others to do the same. Share tips and advice and recommend small action steps to help others practice and improve. Keep track of the work you do and the impact it seems to have on others.

- **Conduct one-on-one or small group training sessions about interpersonal communication.** Ideas include:
  - Changing your approach on-the-fly
  - Listening effectively
  - Dealing with people who refuse to hear what you're saying
  - Understanding body language and why it can be important

  Keep track of the work you do and the impact it seems to have on others.

Behavior 3: Shares Information

Sharing the right information at the right time is crucial to communicating well. People who are skilled at sharing information in a workplace provide information other people need to know to do their jobs. They are timely with information and share and leverage what they know to help others. They are careful not to over-communicate.

Ideas for improving this skill:

- **Become an expert on your content.** The more you know about your subject, the more effective you will be at speaking to it. So spend time studying all sides of an issue, researching the appropriate facts, and preparing for challenges or questions. Interview or speak with subject matter experts for additional data, and crawl content-specific blogs to glean what people are saying across the industry. As you collect data, build an informal fact sheet, and add to it regularly as new information becomes available. Put this approach into practice for the next 60 days, and note how it impacts your ability to easily share necessary information. Later, share your learnings and outcomes with your manager or a trusted advisor.
- **Learn more about what people need from you.** Within the next 30 to 60 days, build a list of the people that you interact with regularly. Interview each person and ask questions like, What kind of information do you need from me? How often do

you need it? How do you like to receive information? What can I do to help you stay better informed? Compare this information to your style and tendencies. What gaps exist? Which individuals seem better informed, and why? Less informed, and why? Make note of your learnings and the outcomes. Later, share this information with your manager or a friend.

- **Deliberately practice rigor in communicating.** Over the next 4 weeks, during key conversations, take these three actions: (1) summarize what has been discussed when appropriate and (2) check for understanding before moving on. Afterward, (3) send out an email detailing each person's next steps and accountabilities, including timelines. Keep track of the instances in which you put this approach into action. What benefits did this rigor yield? Did it save time? Could people act on next steps immediately? Make note of your learnings and the outcomes. Later, share this information with your manager or an advisor.

- **Know your audience.** Know your listeners and consider what appeals to them when preparing to engage. Ask yourself questions like, What is important and or crucial to this person/ group? How do they like to receive information (detailed facts? fun anecdotes? quick and to the point? formal or informal setting?). What is the minimum amount of information they need to be effective? What about my message will get them most excited? Least excited?

  Incorporate the findings of this evaluation into each communication with an eye toward matching and meeting your audience. Over the next 60 days, use your new approach for both formal and informal communications. Keep track of your work in this area, and share your learnings with your manager or a mentor.

- **Practice providing context.** Prior to sharing information, take some time to craft the bigger story behind the communication. Include information about context, end goals, limitations, resources, and vision for success. Ask yourself questions like, What's going on here? Why is this message important? How will this information impact this person or situation 1 year from now? Five years from now? Why is this message important for my target/recipient? How does the recipient of this communication fit into the bigger picture? Put this approach into action for the next 60 days, and note how it impacts your ability to effectively deliver information. Later, share your learnings and outcomes information with your manager or a peer.

- **Develop a system for sharing information.** If you are slow to share information, create a simple system. Try the following two ideas:

  - At the end of each day review your notes from your meetings and conversations, thinking about who needs to know the information. Write that person's name using a bold red pen next to the notes to remind yourself to talk to them (or email them). After you have, cross out their name.

  - If you can, begin each day with a peer "huddle," when you can quickly update everyone at once about news, project updates, and such.

  Commit to trying one of these ideas (or your own) for the next 30 days. Note how your new approach makes it easier to share information. Share your progress with your manager or an advisor.

- **Act as the "information officer" of a cross-functional initiative.** Serve as the informational quarterback between team members and stakeholders. Keep a weekly journal where you record brief entries on the way that you share information. During the life of the project, push yourself to build and circulate team updates, with a focus on keeping people informed on interdependencies; new, relevant developments; and progress to completion. Pay attention to circumstances and situations in which you share information easily and where you struggle, and record your thoughts.

  As the project continues, take steps to improve by anticipating and preparing for conditions in which you have trouble sharing information. After the project, conduct an "information post mortem," and identify what went well with respect to sharing information and what didn't. Keep track of your learnings in this area.

- **Identify the best vehicles for sharing different types of information.** Don't rely on email for everything. For passing along information, asking a simple question, and sharing news with many people at once, email is the way to go. But email isn't appropriate when you need to share difficult news, or when you need input from many people; in these cases face-to-face communication is best. If participants are in different geographic locations, make the extra effort to include them via web conferencing. If face-to-face is impossible, a phone call (or Skype conversation) is the next best option. If you're not sure how to choose the best method for an upcoming communication, list your options, and note the pros and cons of each. Commit to analyzing and trying different methods of sharing information over the next 30 to 60 days. Make note of what works best for you and why. Share your insights and learnings with your manager or a mentor.

- **Use new technology to help share information.** Check out resources such as Dropbox, which enables you to share files and notes through cloud-based storage, or Basecamp, which is a project collaboration tool that includes a message board for group communication. Over the next 30 days, identify and try at least one program that enables you to share information easily.

- **Watch out for information overload.** If you share information regularly and consistently, make sure you aren't overdoing it. Most people need time to process what they've heard before they can accept more. One person may appreciate your input every day, whereas another may perceive that as too much. Over the next 30 to 60 days, check in with the people you work with most often to ask how much information they need. Learn to adjust your delivery to each person's preferences. Share your learnings with your manager or a friend.

- **Take advantage of existing events to share information.** Make a list of all the regular interactions you already have with others, such as group meetings and one-on-ones. Then think about how you can leverage these exchanges to share information with those who need to know. Make notes about what you can share when, and then ask for time on the agenda if necessary. Try this approach for the next 30 days and share your insights with your manager or a trusted advisor.

- **Schedule updates into your project plan or calendar.** As you build project plans, make sure you include a column for Sharing Information, and preschedule the dates that you will provide updates. Then enter these dates in your daily calendar. On a similar note, set aside time each day (or each week) for sharing information, either via emails or phone calls. Over the next 30 to 60 days, implement these techniques to make sharing information a regular habit. Share your progress and insights with your manager or a peer.

- **Read books that provide useful advice for conveying useful information.** Suggestions include:
  - *Communicating Effectively* by *Harvard Business Review*
  - *Mastering Organizational Knowledge Flow: How to Make Knowledge Sharing Work* by Frank Leistner
  - *Knowledge Management Handbook: Collaboration and Social Networking, Second Edition* by Jay Liebowitz

  Dedicate at least 30 minutes a week to reading these resources. For a period of 60 days, make note of the things you learn and new things you would like to try. Review these with your manager or a trusted peer. Discuss how you can incorporate these learnings into your routine.

Ideas for leveraging:

- **Coach people who need help with sharing information.** Review your approach to communicating different types of updates. Share with them your own tips for using email updates most effectively. Interview them about how they tend to update others, and identify places in which they could be more proactive or timely. Meet with them over a period of several weeks.

- **Develop a short presentation about sharing information.** Include tips, best practices, resources, and real-world examples and cases to showcase your experience and knowledge. Topics may include:

- Email versus phone calls versus face-to-face: when to use each vehicle
- How to make updating others a daily habit
- The negative effects of *not* keeping others in the loop

Host a virtual or in-person training session with people who want to develop their skills in this area. As an alternative, share your presentation online: Shoot a short video and post it on YouTube, or create a PowerPoint presentation and post it on your own blog, or on another platform. Keep track of your work in this area.

- **Host a virtual or live lunch-n-learn to discuss sharing information.** Prepare a discussion around how to best keep people in the loop. Discuss technology improvements that can help with team communication. Share past examples of successes and failures and encourage others to do the same. Share tips and advice and recommend small action steps to help others practice and improve. Keep track of the work you do and the impact it seems to have on others.

- **Conduct one-on-one or small group training sessions about sharing information.** Ideas include:
  - Using new online collaboration tools
  - The pros and cons of different delivery methods
  - Writing succinct and effective email updates

Keep track of the work you do and the impact it seems to have on others. Share your activity and learnings with your manager.

Behavior 4: Develops and Delivers Compelling Presentations

Think about the best presentation you have ever seen. What made it successful? People who develop and deliver compelling presentations create coherent and convincing presentations using technology effectively to enhance the experience for the audience. They present with authority, poise, and confidence. They command attention and can manage the group process during the presentation.

Ideas for improving this skill:

- **Know your audience.** Before making a presentation, think carefully about who will be in your audience. Make yourself an audience analysis checklist that includes these questions:

    o Is your audience made up of peers, direct reports, those in higher positions, or a mix of the two?

    o What do they already know about the subject?

    o Will your audience be receptive to or skeptical/resistant to your information?

    o How much time has been allotted for the presentation?

    o What are your audience's priorities? What are their main obstacles?

    o Have they recently been through major changes or difficulties? What other situational context may be relevant?

    The answers to these questions can help you craft messages with the language, information, and tone that are right for your particular audience. For example, if you know your audience will be inclined to be opposed to your information, you need to be empathetic yet persuasive. If your audience sees your message as just more work for them, you need to clearly spell out the benefits of the work. Use the preceding questions as your audience analysis checklist for the next 30 days. Note how it helps you prepare your messaging. Share your progress and insights with your manager or a friend.

- **Anticipate your audience's questions.** When planning your next presentation, make a list of every possible question or objection your audience may have. Ensure you have well-thought-out answers; or better yet, be proactive and weave the answers to the anticipated questions into the body of your presentation. Try this approach for the next 30 to 60 days, and note the difference in how your presentations are received. Share your progress with your manager or a mentor.

- **Be clear about your purpose and your point of view.** Take the time upfront to carefully decide on the purpose of the presentation: Is it to inform? To entertain? To convince your audience to do something (or to stop doing something)? Consider what you want to accomplish and the impression you want to convey. Will a strong, logical argument work best? Or would an anecdotal personal appeal be a better approach?

For the next 60 days, consider these questions before you begin creating your presentation. Write your purpose and the results you want on Post-it® Notes and place them on your computer screen as you create your presentation. These visual reminders can help you write a presentation that stays on track with your goals. Note how this approach affects the effectiveness of your presentations, and share the results with your manager or a trusted advisor.

- **Create an organized outline around your key messages.** A good outline is necessary to ensure that your presentation makes sense and flows well. For the next 60 days, begin your presentations with an organized approach. Sketch out the body of your presentation, including:
  - Your purpose
  - Your introduction
  - Your key messages (no more than five)
  - Your conclusion, including a call for action

  Take time to call out your key messages before you begin writing. Keep in mind that each key message should address just one idea. You'll probably have too many details and a lot of information that you could include, but limit yourself to just the high-level messages that will drive your points home. Show your outline to a trusted peer before you begin to flesh out the content. At the end of 60 days, note how this approach helped you build more powerful presentations. Share your insights with your manager or a mentor.

- **Make your introduction matter.** The introduction to your presentation sets the stage for what's about to follow—and it's also when your audience forms its first impression of you. A good introduction should do three things:

1. Capture your audience's attention. Ways to do this:
   - A dramatic quote or statement that relates to your topic
   - Asking a question about your topic that requires a response from the audience
   - Showing a dramatic photo or illustration that relates to your topic
   - Telling a topic-related story or anecdote from your own experience
2. Provide necessary context or background information.
3. Introduce your purpose and the key messages that support it.

   Some hypothetical examples:
   - "By the end of this presentation, you will see why I believe that pens are better than pencils: They are permanent; they come in different colors; and they are more legible."
   - "Today I am going to tell you about the upcoming change we're making in our vendor selection: why we're making the change, how it will affect you, and when it will be effective."

For the next 60 days, commit to spending extra time creating powerful introductions for your presentations. Practice them in front of your family or friends and get their feedback. Did you grab their interest? Do they understand what they're about to hear about? Note how this extra effort helped you make better presentations, and share your insights with your manager or a friend.

- **Practice the skill of audience interaction.** Knowing how to keep your audience engaged is part of giving a great presentation. Over the next 60 days, focus on these two skills during your presentations:
  - *Allow for audience questions.* Decide on how you want to handle questions from your audience during your presentation. Do you want them to ask you throughout or wait until the end? Tell your audience upfront which you prefer. Be sure to build enough time (10 minutes or so) into your presentation for this exchange.

o *Learn to handle disagreements.* During the next month, watch how others manage to diffuse conflict during group discussions and make note of what you learn. Use role-plays with friends to practice these techniques for getting the conversation back on track until you have mastered them. Then, be prepared for disagreements or conflict during your presentation by anticipating where the "hot spots" might be and planning your responses as much as possible.

Make note of your progress and key learnings, and share them with your manager or a mentor.

- **Craft a concrete conclusion.** Your conclusion should be brief but powerful. Include:

  o A quick recap of your key messages

  o A clear picture of why your audience should do what you want them to do ("what's in it for me")

  o A clear call to action

  Over the next 60 days, take time to actually write out the conclusions to each presentation you create; don't just assume that you can create them on-the-fly. Practice them in front of a mirror or a friend. Did you remind the audience of your purpose? Did you engage, inspire, or entertain them? If not, keep working on it until you feel ready. Share your learnings and progress with your manager or a peer.

- **Learn when and how to use slides and other audiovisual aids.** Do not assume that you must have a slide for every point you make. In fact, in most presentations, the fewer slides the better. Take time to observe how others use slides during their presentations. Do you find it more effective as an audience member when there are fewer slides, or more? How else do others illustrate their points? Consider such aspects as:

  o Use key words instead of whole sentences.

  o Choose a font that is easy to read and large enough to be read across the room.

  o Be consistent with the style of font, color, and such throughout all slides.

- o Use the 1x5x5 rule: no more than five words per line; no more than five lines per slide.
- **In addition, look for and assess the use by others of alternative audiovisuals such as:**
  - o Showing a photograph when describing a place
  - o Holding up a sample of a product
  - o Showing a map to illustrate distance between places
  - o Playing music or snippets of podcasts to illustrate your points

  Be willing to experiment with these types of audiovisual aids.

  Over the next 60 days, make note of what you observe, what you try, and what works best for you. Ask your peers to give you feedback on your slides and other audiovisuals. Note your progress as you implement these techniques. Share your key learnings and insights with your manager or a peer.

- **Improve the way you use data in presentations.** Over the next 60 days, try these techniques to improve the way you present data in your presentations.
  - o *Listen to presentations or read reports that you find helpful and understandable.* How do they present data? How do they explain complex terms? One of the most effective ways to improve your use of financial data is to learn how others present it effectively.
  - o *Present data visually.* It is easier to make sense of visual displays than lists of numbers. Make effective use of charts and graphs, and use the format that best supports your key messages. For example, pie charts illustrate relative proportions, line graphs show changes over time, and bar charts compare targets.
  - o *Avoid highly complex graphics.* Do not attempt to put complicated flow charts or diagrams on a slide. Your audience will become frustrated and lose interest. Find a better way to represent the information. If you must share a complex graphic, include it as a handout at the end of the presentation instead of putting it into the body of your presentation.

Ask your peers to give you feedback on your data slides and note your progress as you implement these techniques. Share your insights with your manager or a trusted advisor.

- **Polish your presentation skills.** Over the next 60 days, commit to practicing your presentations in front of a video camera. Ask your friends or family to watch as well and give you feedback on the following:
  - How well you connect with your audience
  - The tone and volume of your voice
  - Your ability to facilitate the conversation and keep it on track
  - How well you deliver a clear call to action
  - How your information is organized
  - The impact and clarity of your PowerPoint slides (when appropriate)
  - Use of vocabulary; how articulate you are
  - Your pace and use of pauses
  - The smoothness of your transitions from one point to another
  - The length of your presentation

  Make note of your areas for improvement, and then practice again. Continue to revise your presentation and practice until you feel comfortable with your content *and* your delivery. Note how your confidence improves as you practice, and share your progress with your manager or a mentor.

- **Watch your nonverbal cues.** Ask a trusted peer to watch your body language when you're communicating. Better yet, ask them to video you in an unobtrusive way. Later, discuss your style with them: Do you look receptive? Are your arms crossed or relaxed? What expression is on your face? Make notes about three things you'll do differently about your nonverbal communication and commit to implementing them over the next 30 days. Share your insights with your manager or a trusted advisor.

- **Join a presentation skills group.** Consider participating in a Toastmasters group to increase your skills in connecting with a variety of audiences (who want and expect different things) to get the results you want. See www.toastmasters.org for more information. Share what you are learning with peers as the class progresses.

- **Read books that provide useful presentation skills and advice.** Suggestions include:
  - ○ *The Presentation Secrets of Steve Jobs: How to Be Insanely Great in Front of Any Audience* by Carmine Gallo
  - ○ *The Exceptional Presenter: A Proven Formula to Open Up and Own the Room* by Timothy J. Koegel
  - ○ *slide:ology: The Art and Science of Creating Great Presentations* by Nancy Duarte

Dedicate at least 30 minutes a week to reading these resources. For a period of 60 days, make note of the things you learn and new things you would like to try. Review these with a trusted peer or your manager. Discuss how you can incorporate these learnings into your routine.

Ideas for leveraging:

- **Coach people who need help with their presentation skills.** Review your approach to planning for different types of presentations. Share with them your tips for making your presentations pop, as well as potential pitfalls to avoid. Review their presentation outlines before they finalize them, and share your feedback (and logic) with them. Watch them make presentations, and identify places in which they could have been clearer, more succinct, and more. Meet with them over a period of several weeks.

- **Develop a short presentation about presenting in front of a group.** Include tips, best practices, resources, and real-world examples and cases to showcase your experience and knowledge. Topics may include:
  - ○ Creating great introductions and conclusions
  - ○ Developing your key messages
  - ○ Varying your tone of voice for impact
  - ○ The top five most common presentation mistakes

Host a virtual or in-person training session with people who want to become better presenters. As an alternative, share your presentation online: Shoot a short video and post it on You-Tube, or create a PowerPoint presentation and post it on your own blog, or on another platform. Keep track of your work in this area.

- **Host a virtual or live lunch-n-learn to discuss presentation tips.** Prepare a discussion around creating effective presentations. Discuss common problems that people face, such as weak introductions or busy, ineffective slides. Share past examples of successes and failures and encourage others to do the same. Share tips and advice and recommend small action steps to help others practice and improve. Keep track of the work you do and the impact it seems to have on others.

- **Offer to be someone's warm-up audience.** Help others improve their presentation skills by offering to watch their presentations before they deliver them to their official audience. Take the time to review your feedback, explaining the logic behind your comments. Give them two to three simple things they can do for immediate improvement. Keep track of the work you do, and the impact you feel it's having on others.

Behavior 5: Collaborates Across Boundaries

In today's work world, it's increasingly common for employees to work across boundaries of culture and location. Working with people in different locations presents opportunities to expand the talent and resources you have available to you and your work. It can also be challenging because it's not easy to observe people, and you might not have easy access to the people you work with. Someone who collaborates well across boundaries takes care to build trust and communicate clearly with peers in other locations.

Ideas for improving this skill:

- **Join a virtual group that reflects an interest or hobby of yours; for example, a LinkedIn professional group, a Facebook group, or take an online class.** Spend 30 days participating in the group and notice what about your experience is easy or enjoyable, and what aspects are more challenging. What is the best approach to communicating with the others in your group? Share your learnings with your manager or a friend.

- **Become familiar with and practice using virtual collaboration tools.** There are many tools to help teams work together from a distance. Try a free tool or sign up for a free trial and work with family members or friends in different locations to solve a problem or plan an event or project, like a reunion. This will familiarize you with the tool and the process, and give you firsthand experience working toward a goal with a virtual team. The website Capterra offers a list of collaboration tools to explore at www.capterra.com (search Collaboration Software). Share your experience and key learnings with your manager or a trusted advisor.

- **Remember the differences in time zones, and plan accordingly.** When working with people in different geographic locations, clarify which time zone you mean for every written or spoken time or date. Be especially aware of time differences when setting deadlines, keeping in mind that one region's Thursday morning can be another region's Thursday night or even Friday morning.

- **Ensure clear roles and goals.** These are more important than ever within a virtual team because daily interaction and ongoing clarification are not always possible. Within the next 30 days, ensure that you know your specific role and expectations within the virtual community you joined or virtual project you are working on, and that you understand the roles and goals of all other team members as well. Share your learnings and progress with your manager or a friend.

- **Make communication a priority.** Because you can't just drop in on a team member in another location, you need to develop new habits for keeping in touch. Over the next 30 days, commit to a regular scheduled time for communication with each team member. Vary your communication approaches to include emails, Skype calls, phone calls, and instant messages to see what works best. Share your learnings with your manager or a peer.

Learn to effectively facilitate virtual meetings. Some tips to keep in mind follow:

○ When planning your agenda, put items that pertain to all first, so others can leave the call if necessary.

○ Do your best to schedule meetings when everyone can attend, no matter where they're located. For regular calls it's a good idea to rotate the time zones so that everyone has the early morning and evening advantage.

○ Choose the best type of meeting technology for your needs. Do you need to see faces or documents? If so, you might arrange a Skype call. In other cases, a conference call will suffice.

○ At the beginning of a conference call, be sure to name everyone attending, either in the room or on the phone. Institute a "warm-up" at the beginning of the meeting, where participants check in with a brief anecdote about a recent event in their life. This warm-up enables non-native English speakers to get in the swing of speaking English, and it also allows all team members to get to know one another and build trust.

○ Speak loudly and slowly, and identify yourself each time you speak during conference calls.

• **Keep cultural communication differences in mind.** Within the next 30 to 60 days, learn about cultural communication differences and how they can affect the team. For example:

○ Some cultures prefer direct and explicit communication, whereas others prefer more indirect methods.

○ Words can have different meanings across English-speaking countries.

○ Each location has its own jargon and shortcuts that people from other locations won't understand.

○ Document what you learn, and choose the top five most important tips. Share them with your manager or a friend.

- **Read books that offer insightful strategies for global collaboration.** Suggestions include:
  - *Virtual Teamwork: Mastering the Art and Practice of Online Learning and Corporate Collaboration* by Robert Ubell, Jerry Hultin, and Frank Mayadas
  - *Rocket: A Simulation on Intercultural Teamwork* by Jessica Hirshorn
  - *Virtual Team Success: A Practical Guide for Working and Leading from a Distance* by Richard Lepsinger and Darleen DeRosa

  Dedicate at least 30 minutes a week to reading these resources. For a period of 60 days, make note of the things you learn and new things you would like to try. Review these with a trusted peer or your manager. Discuss how you can incorporate these learnings into your routine.

Ideas for leveraging:

- **Coach people who need to build relationships and expand their network.** Review your approach to meeting new people and building your network. Share your logic behind developing contacts in other departments and companies. Help them identify why they feel uncomfortable doing so. Offer to attend a networking event with them and coach them as they develop new contacts. Meet with them over a period of several weeks.

- **Develop a short presentation about the people within your dispersed team.** Create a "live yearbook" that includes photos and video interviews with team members from all locations. Make it your goal for every team member to feel known and appreciated. If possible, share your presentation in person. For those who aren't in the same location as you, put your presentation online: Post it on YouTube, or create a PowerPoint presentation and post it on your own blog, or on another platform. Gather feedback from team members.

- **Develop a video blog (vlog) for your team.** As a way to increase visual communication within your dispersed team, create a monthly vlog that enables all members to share news, stories, and successes "in person" (even if not in real time). Arrange for other locations to shoot their own episodes as well. Get feedback and ideas from your teammates.

- **Become your team's technical guru.** Keep up-to-date with the latest technology designed to make virtual team collaboration easier and more effective. Subscribe to blogs and sites dedicated to this type of technology. Offer to try new programs and resources and compare them to what your team is already using. Train other team members to use the technology more efficiently, either one-on-one or through group meetings or webinars.

Behavior 6: Adopts a Cross-Cultural Mindset

The diversity of people in our country grows every day, and the ability to work with and learn from others different from ourselves is increasingly important. People who adopt a cross-cultural mindset are role models in seeking and respecting diverse perspectives and contributions. At work, they recognize and address the complexities associated with being part of a global team. They seek to understand cultures and norms that are different than their own.

Ideas for improving this skill:

- **Seek diverse perspectives on a difficult problem.** Identify a complex and persistent problem, and seek input from a diverse group of people (race, level, function, background, and such). Use a grid to track the different perspectives, as well as anything unique that you learned from each perspective. Leverage the grid when developing the solution for the problem. Later, reflect on how the solution would have been different and less effective had you not collected input from a diverse group. Commit to implementing this plan within the next 30 to 60 days. Record your findings and share your learnings with your manager or a trusted advisor.

- **Build and leverage a diverse network.** Your ability to appreciate and leverage diversity of all kinds can depend upon the breadth of your network. Evaluate your network with a critical eye: How diverse is it? What gaps exist? How many people in your network typically have views different from your own? Push yourself to grow the diversity of your network. Look across cultures, ethnicities, industries, socio-economic backgrounds, ages, and pay-grade to find people who can offer unique insight and new ways of thinking through things. When you meet new people, strike up a conversation to learn about their interests or line of work. Send LinkedIn messages or invitations to connect to interesting people, and talk with them over coffee. As you ask them about themselves, think about how their approaches or ideas could possibly be applied to your life or work. Track your efforts over the next 30 to 60 days and then share your learnings with your manager or a trusted peer.

- **Learn about and make notes on the diversity in those around you.** Appreciate the diversity in those around you and catalogue the ways in which your friends or co-workers are diverse. As a thought exercise, make a list of everything diverse about your immediate work group. Remember that diversity is not limited to skin color, race, or sexual orientation! Do you have a co-worker who participates in an unusual sport or has an interesting hobby? Include anything that makes these individuals different and valuable as part of your team. Also note similarities among your peers. Add additional information about these individuals as you get to know them better. Reflect on how this diversity positively impacts your life. Make notes over 30 days, and then share your insights with your manager or a friend.

- **Attend an affiliation group meeting.** If your organization, place of worship, or school has an affiliation group for a diverse population that you may or may not belong to, attend a few of their meetings. Is there a group for professional women in your organization? African-Americans? Families with dual-career spouses? Parents or children with disabilities? Find a group that you would not otherwise join and attend meetings as an ally. Listen to the group's concerns and values to find some common ground and shared experiences. Keep notes on upcoming events and share your findings with your manager or a mentor.

- **Examine your own discomfort.** If working with people from backgrounds different than yours makes you uncomfortable, assess your own attitudes, assumptions, and feelings about other ethnicities and cultures. Did you previously have a negative interaction that is influencing your attitude? Are you unconsciously letting stereotypes affect you? Do you lack exposure to certain types of cultures or ethnicities? You must understand your own beliefs to change them. Over the next 30 to 60 days, make notes about your self-reflection. Share your insights with your manager or a trusted peer and ask for their own perceptions. When you are ready, commit to trying at least one technique to bolster your appreciation of, and comfort with, other cultures.

- **Learn about other cultures.** Increase your exposure to those who are different to you. Over the next 30 to 60 days, read about and talk to people from different backgrounds. Share a meal with someone from another ethnicity, or watch a foreign film. Do whatever you can to increase your understanding of other cultures' values, norms, and customs so they become less mysterious, threatening, or foreign to you. Share your insights with your manager or a friend.

- **Put yourself in unfamiliar situations.** Go to meetings or gatherings that aren't related to your interests. Have lunch with someone you don't know well. Join a club or organization that focuses on something you are unfamiliar with. Practice working through your discomfort and learning from new perspectives. Consider that people from other cultures might feel this sense of unfamiliarity and discomfort every day at work. How might you help them adjust and adapt? How did others help you when you were out of your comfort zone? Make note of your insights over the course of a month, and share them with your manager or an advisor.

- **Assess, and challenge, your personal biases.** Consider if you have a tendency to favor people who think, look, and act like you. Which specific characteristics do you tend to overvalue? Brainstorm and write down the consequences of 'sequestering' yourself in this way: both negatives and positives.

Now consider which characteristics you tend to avoid, judge, or trivialize. Identify them specifically. Practice observing people who exhibit these, and look for the ways in which these characteristics make them effective. What can you learn from them? How can increase your interactions with them? Put this plan into action over the next 30 to 60 days, and make note of your observations. Share your learnings with your manager or a peer.

- **Read books that delve into developing a cross-cultural mindset.** Suggestions include:
  - *Kiss, Bow, or Shake Hands: The Bestselling Guide to Doing Business in More than 60 Countries* by Terri Morrison and Wayne A. Conaway
  - *Cross-Cultural Dialogues: 74 Brief Encounters with Cultural Difference* by Craig Storti
  - *The Cultural Intelligence Difference: Master the One Skill You Can't Do Without in Today's Global Economy* by David Livermore Ph.D.
  - *When Cultures Collide: Leading Across Cultures* by Richard D. Lewis

Dedicate at least 30 minutes a week to reading these resources. For a period of 60 days, make note of the things you learn and new things you would like to try. Review these with your manager or a trusted peer. Discuss how you can incorporate these learnings into your routine.

Ideas for leveraging:

- **Coach people who need help in appreciating different cultures.** Review your approach to learning about and appreciating people who are different than you. Share your tips for identifying and overcoming your own biases. Help them build their network to include a variety of ages, ethnicities, and backgrounds. Introduce them to others. Meet with them over a period of several weeks to discuss experiences and insights. Alternatively, mentor an individual from a different country or culture who seeks to be successful in his career here. Work together over several weeks to help him identify, understand,

and navigate through cultural differences. In either case, assess how effectively you coach, and share your activities and learnings with your manager or a peer.

- **Develop a short presentation showcasing the diversity within your organization.** Share statistics about the different cultures within your workforce and the different languages spoken. Include photos and video clips of interviews from a variety of people from different locations within your organization. Do your best to illustrate what a "global organization" looks, sounds, and thinks like. Show your presentation to your team, and offer to share it across your organization.

- **Host a virtual or live lunch-n-learn to discuss the importance of cultivating diversity within an organization.** Prepare a discussion around how and why diversity of cultures, ethnicities, and sexual orientations is critical to an organization's success. Share past examples of diversity "blunders" and encourage others to do the same. Find out what other organizations or teams are doing to take advantage of the differences among team members. Keep track of the work you do and the impact it seems to have on others.

- **Create a guest-speaker series for your team.** Offer to find and recruit people who represent different cultures and perspectives, and organize a quarterly speaker series. Invite speakers with wildly divergent backgrounds, so your team will be exposed to completely new ways of seeing the world. Encourage team members to ask questions.

6

Competency: Demonstrates Personal Excellence

Behavior 1: Demonstrates Integrity

Behavior 2: Relishes Accountability

Behavior 3: Exhibits Intellectual Curiosity

Behavior 4: Develops Self

Overview of Competency

Think of someone you trust and admire. What qualities do they have that make you view them in that way? People who exhibit personal excellence have integrity and are trustworthy. They can be counted on to do the right thing in any situation, and they willingly take responsibility for their actions. They gain insights from mistakes and are open to criticism and feedback. They are self-aware and strive to improve their own skills and to learn continuously. They follow through on commitments and model a service orientation toward others.

Behavior 1: Demonstrates Integrity

What does it mean to demonstrate integrity? People with integrity can be counted on to do the right thing in any situation. They keep confidences and readily admit mistakes. They are direct and truthful. They make ethical judgments in all cases and have a strong moral compass. In demonstrating these behaviors, they fuel relationships of growing trust and mutual respect.

Ideas for improving this skill:

- **Match your actions with your words.** People pay attention to what you do more than what you say, so show them that you are trustworthy. Over the next 30 days, take extra steps to build trust with those around you. Use the following guidelines:

  - *Keep your promises.* Do what you say you are going to do.

  - *Keep it to yourself.* If someone has told you something in confidence, do not share it with anyone else.

  - *Deliver feedback, even when it's tough.* Present the unvarnished truth when necessary in an appropriate and helpful manner. Show empathy for others' feelings as you share feedback that they need to know.

  These steps can help you develop a reputation as someone who is honest and ethical. Keep track of your efforts and share them with your manager or a trusted advisor.

- **Consistently honor your personal commitments.** Honoring commitments is integral to demonstrating integrity. Be thoughtful about what commitments you make. Try one or more of the following techniques to bolster how others perceive you in this area:

  - When you make a commitment, follow it through every time. Consider writing it down and marking it on your calendar to help you remember.

  - Avoid making statements that could be interpreted as a commitment. For example, saying, "I'll try to do that by Monday" could be interpreted as a commitment.

  - If you fail to keep a promise, make sure to give advance warning, and then follow up and apologize. Don't let it slide or assume it's not a big deal.

  - Take time to address the concerns people bring to you and offer a thoughtful realistic solution or timeline that you are sure you can meet.

  - Keep personal information confidential. If you are unclear about confidentiality, ask upfront, "Is this to be kept confidential?" Clarify who has access to the information and who can be privy to it as you pursue your goals.

Put two to three of these techniques into action over the next 60 days. Keep track of your progress and share the outcome with your manager or a trusted friend.

- **Explore how your favorite organization lives its values.** Review the organization's values. If possible, interview someone from the organization. Ask questions like, What does this value look like in action? How do you leverage an understanding of the values when making decisions? What are some challenges that you and other employees have faced with respect to living the values? Reflect on your learnings with your manager or an advisor.

- **Create your own personal values statement that reflects the way you want to live and work.** By what standards do you make decisions? To what philosophies or mantras do you subscribe? Carve out some time to create this document and post it somewhere you'll see it. For the next 30 days, record the decisions you have made and to what degree the decisions reflect your code. Which decisions were most difficult to make? Why? How might others perceive your decisions? Did they appear to be in line with what those around you think of you, or would some surprise them? Why? Discuss your learnings with your manager or a mentor.

- **Take responsibility by admitting mistakes.** Admit the mistake early and inform everyone affected so they're aware. If necessary, publicly acknowledge the mistake and take personal responsibility. Let people know what you plan to do to correct the situation and how you will keep the mistake from happening again. Then, take some time to reflect on the mistake and how you handled it. What did you learn from the mistake? How can you keep it from happening again? How did people respond to your attempt to take accountability for the mistake? Put this approach into action for the next 90 days. Reflect on your progress and share your learnings and outcomes with your manager or a trusted advisor.

- **Rectify a previous error.** Ask a trusted peer, mentor, or your supervisor to give you feedback on a project that did not go well. What could you improve in the future? Were there steps that you could have taken to mitigate problems outside of your immediate control? What can you do now to rectify the previous issue? If applicable, make a plan to rectify the issue and commit to addressing it in the next 60 days. If not, identify an opportunity to incorporate the feedback into a current project. Keep track of your learnings and share them with your manager or a friend.

- **Demonstrate courage to call out unethical behavior.** You have an obligation to speak up if you see something at work or in your life that is unethical. If this feels uncomfortable to you, try these methods:
  - At work, familiarize yourself with your organization's standards of conduct. Identify what rule or value you believe is being breached. Note the proper channels to take to report the issue.
  - Find a coach or role model who can help you learn to be more assertive in general. Study how assertive people start discussions, deal with interruptions, express their views, and respond to criticism.
  - Practice clearly stating your point of view directly and confidently, especially when you're in safe environments, interacting with those close to you. Keep a journal of when you try this—both within and outside of work—and review this with your manager or a mentor to demonstrate your progress.

  Keep track of the instances in which you put these approaches into action. Make note of your learnings and the outcomes. Later, share this information with a trusted friend.

- **Find a personal mentor who represents integrity to you.** Within the next 30 to 60 days, identify someone whom you believe demonstrates the highest ethical behavior. Ask to meet with them on a regular basis. Ask questions such as, How do ethical judgments affect your decisions? Have you ever had to go against your better judgment? What was the outcome? Have you ever had to call out unethical behavior in someone else? How did you do it? Make note of what you learn, and consider how you can apply some of these learnings to your own work. Share your insights with your manager or a peer.

- **Read books that focus on maintaining and exemplifying integrity.** Suggestions include:
  - *Character Counts: The Power of Personal Integrity* by Charles H. Dyer and Charles R. Swindoll
  - *Business Ethics: Decision Making for Personal Integrity & Social Responsibility* by Laura Hartman and Joseph DesJardins
  - *Absolute Honesty: Building a Corporate Culture That Values Straight Talk and Rewards Integrity* by Larry Johnson and Bob Phillips

  Dedicate at least 30 minutes a week to reading these resources. For a period of 60 days, make note of the things you learn and new things you would like to try. Review these with your manager or a trusted peer. Discuss how you can incorporate these learnings into your routine.

Ideas for leveraging:

- **Coach people who want to demonstrate greater integrity.** Review your organization's values and help them understand what they mean. Share your approach to making ethical decisions in your work and include real-life examples and situations. Interview them about times that they have misjudged people or problems, and suggest your ideas for what they could have done differently. Coach them on how to improve in demonstrating integrity and share your thinking and feedback regularly. Meet with them throughout the process to review their thoughts and concerns. Keep track of your activities and learnings in this area.

- **Host a virtual or live lunch-n-learn to discuss the importance of integrity and ethics within organizations.** Prepare a discussion around values, making tough calls, and social responsibility. Use past examples of successes and failures and encourage others to do the same. Share tips and advice and recommend small action steps to help others practice and improve. Keep track of the work you do and the impact it seems to have on others.

- **Develop a short presentation reviewing your organiza-tion's values.** Find real-life examples of the values in action, and include profiles of people who demonstrate integrity. Host a virtual or in-person session with people who want to improve in this area. As an alternative, share your presentation online: Shoot a short video and post it on YouTube, or create a Power-Point presentation and post it on your own blog, or on another platform. Keep track of your work in this area.

  Conduct one-on-one or small group training sessions about demonstrating integrity. Topics might include the following:

  - Taking full accountability for self
  - How to deliver tough feedback with honesty and clarity
  - Making and managing commitments
  - Living your (or your organization's) values

  Ask for feedback from participants. Share your agendas and results with your manager or a trusted advisor.

Behavior 2: Relishes Accountability

People who relish accountability willingly take responsibility for their actions. They do not make excuses and they own their successes and failures. They seek out new and different responsibilities and demonstrate confidence in their ability to deliver on results. They follow through on commitments and hold others accountable as well.

Ideas for improving this skill:

- **Demonstrate accountability and follow through.** Within the next 60 days, introduce these guidelines into your life:

  - Follow through with commitments on or before schedule. Be focused and committed to doing what you say you're going to do when you say you're going to do it. Make note of the commitments you make and whether you follow through on them. Communicate with those around you who are impacted by what you do and let them know your progress.

  - Complete tasks or assignments early. Push yourself and plan your time to complete tasks before they are due.

○ Set a time frame for resolving issues and requests that you receive. Set deadlines for gathering information and implementing a solution. Record these dates on your calendar and commit to meeting them.

Keep track of your work in this area and share your learnings with your manager or a trusted advisor.

• **Own feedback—even the tough stuff.** Show that you are accountable by owning the feedback you receive. Try these tips:

○ *Keep all excuses out of the conversation.* Refrain from finger pointing, defensive posturing, and defensive questions and contradicting language ("but," "you know," and more). Although you will not always agree with all feedback (and you shouldn't), push yourself to listen to feedback without rebutting.

○ *Don't blame others.* If you consistently blame someone else for your own mistakes, you will alienate yourself from others. Instead, take a deep breath and admit what you could have done differently. Focus on what you have learned from the mistake instead of dwelling on the mistake itself. People will appreciate your honesty and will therefore be likely to trust you in the future.

○ *View failure as a chance to learn.* Instead of thinking about mistakes as failure, see them as opportunities to learn. Analyze your error, either by yourself or with a peer. Make note of what you can do differently next time. Remember, mistakes are only a problem if you repeat them or don't learn from them.

○ *Give up on perfection.* You may be afraid of owning up to your mistakes because you've set unrealistic expectations for yourself. It's a cliché that bears repeating: No one is perfect. Study the most successful people you know, and eventually you'll see that they also make mistakes sometimes. However, they are successful because they acknowledge their errors, learn from them, and move on. The next time you make a mistake, try giving yourself a break. You'll see that accepting and learning from your occasional blunders is much more productive than ignoring them.

Put these guidelines into action for the next 60 days and record your findings. Later, share your learnings and outcomes with your manager or a friend.

- **Perform a self-assessment on a major project.** Before seeking feedback from others on an important project, take the initiative to perform your own self-assessment of the work. Is it complete? Are there gaping holes that you should try to fill before seeking feedback from others? Be honest and harsh in your self-criticism, but also find strategies to bolster your success. When your project is ready for feedback, share it with others and compare their reactions to your self-assessment. Put this plan into action within the next 60 days.

- **Practice questioning techniques to drive accountable action in yourself.** When faced with a situation in which your actions or work were not up to standards, or where there was room for improvement, consider these questions:

  - In what areas could the results or outcome be improved? Look for observable and concrete data and behaviors.

  - What is the performance gap? What was my actual performance and how does it compare with the expected performance?

  - What did I do well that I want to continue in my future work?

  - How well did I interact with others?

  - What were the major causes of the problem? How did I contribute to the situation?

  - What could have been done differently to prevent the outcome? Have I done all that is possible?

  - What needs to happen right now to achieve a more desirable outcome?

  - What can I do next time to prevent what occurred from happening again? How can I apply this learning to other tasks?

In the next 30 days, identify two or three situations in which you can use these questioning techniques. Reflect on what you learned and how you will respond differently going forward. Share what you have learned with your manager or a mentor and ask for feedback.

- **Identify a person in your organization who models personal accountability and ask him/her for informal coaching.** Spend some time shadowing this person and observing the behaviors or techniques she uses with herself and others that instill ownership and accountability. Ask her to share techniques she uses, the situations in which she uses them, and the impact. Inquire about a work situation in her past where the results did not work out as well as she had hoped. Explore what she learned from the situation and what she does differently today as a result. Ask her to share how she identifies her own improvement opportunities. Make note of your observations and list techniques that you will incorporate into your own approach. Try putting one or more of these approaches into action over the next 90 days. Later, share your learnings and outcomes with your manager or a trusted friend.

- **Take responsibility quickly when a problem arises.** The next time people approach you with a problem or complaint, get in front of the issue; don't avoid it. As soon as the problem surfaces, explore the issue by asking probing questions. Allow them to explain what happened, what their expectations are, and what they need from you. Identify the desired outcome and the best way to reach it. Follow up on action items quickly and communicate to all who are involved in the situation. Notice how proactive, accountable action can diffuse an unwanted situation. Put this technique into action over the next 30 to 60 days. Keep track of your work and share your learnings and outcomes with your manager or a peer.

- **Flex accountability by analyzing past mistakes.** Document the last few situations in which the outcome was less than desirable, but you had previously claimed was "out of your control."

Reflect on each of these experiences and push yourself to take accountability for the unwanted outcome. Ask yourself questions like, What could I have done to encourage a better outcome? If I had been fully responsible for the outcome, how would I have managed it differently? What would a perfect outcome have looked like, and how could I have supported that outcome? When did I know that we were headed down the wrong path, and what could I have done to help steer the situation in the right direction? Reflect on your findings. What themes emerge? Identify some techniques and approaches you want to adopt to increase accountability going forward and implement over the next 60 days. Review your learnings and outcomes with your manager or a mentor.

- **Leverage small actions to build accountability and ownership.** Consider the little things you do throughout the day that demonstrate accountability. Track your effectiveness in these three areas:
  - Returning phone calls and emails the same day of receipt
  - Scheduling meetings effectively to arrive on time and to avoid having to cancel meetings due to overbooking
  - Leaving short interims between appointments to allow for meetings that may run overtime and to provide lead-time to get to and from appointments
  - Following up when appropriate
  - Keeping promises and commitments; doing what you say you will do

For the next 30 days, take a few moments in the evening to review your day. Note how many times you kept your commitments in these areas and note situations in which you did not. Look at what interfered or kept you from keeping a commitment. What was the root cause? How could you adjust how you plan your day to decrease the likelihood of that event from recurring? Note your progress and share this with your manager or a friend.

- **Create monthly goals, weekly tasks, and daily action plans.** At the start of the month, identify two or three goals that you will complete within 30 days. Outline action items or tasks that need to occur each week to reach your goal and assign an estimated time for completion of each task. Finally, create a daily action plan or to-do list. Review the list at the start of your workday and schedule times on your calendar for task completion. Monitor the list at least two or three times throughout the day. Review again in the evening identifying the tasks that have been completed and those that were not accomplished and why. Be proactive by creating your action plan for the next day. Follow this plan for an entire month, and note your progress. Share your learnings with your manager or a trusted advisor.

- **Exceed a major goal.** In the next 30 days, identify a goal and determine steps that you can take to turn a good performance into an excellent performance. Self-evaluate and set goals above the ones that are expected of you. Brainstorm ways that you can make your deliverable more effective, cheaper, and ahead of schedule and plan your priorities accordingly. Afterward, reflect on the experience. What did you learn? What will you incorporate into your approach going forward? Take it a step further by seeking feedback from others. Later, share your learnings and outcomes with your manager or a mentor.

- **Rectify a previous error.** Over the next month, ask a trusted peer or mentor to give you feedback on a project that did not go well. What could you improve for the future? Were there steps that you could have taken to mitigate problems outside of your immediate control? Is there something you can do now to rectify the previous issue? If so, make a plan to resolve the problem and commit to addressing it in the next 60 days. If not, identify an opportunity to incorporate the feedback into a current project. Keep track of your learnings and share them with your manager or a friend.

- **Use language that demonstrates accountability.** Over the next month, pay attention to the words that you and others around you use and that imply ownership or lack of ownership.

Lack of Ownership: Phrases That Complain or Blame	Ownership: Action-Oriented and Accountable Phrases
It's not my fault.	This was my part.
It's not my job.	This is what I can do.
I tried.	This is what I will do.
You should; he should; they should.	It will work when I.
They did it; he/she did it; you did it.	I choose to.
Why didn't you? Why didn't they?	I choose not to.
I can't.	I can.
I have to.	I will.
When you.	When I.
	I always.

Notice which words you use most often for 60 days. Then consciously focus your efforts on consistently using words that reinforce ownership. Notice the impact the language has on you. Monitor yourself to see if you are increasing the use of action-oriented, accountable language. Share your findings with your manager or a friend.

- **Read books that inspire honesty, integrity and accountability.** Suggestions include:
  - *Accountability: The Key to Driving a High-Performance Culture* by Greg Bustin
  - *Crucial Accountability: Tools for Resolving Violated Expectations, Broken Commitments, and Bad Behavior* by Kerry Patterson, Joseph Grenny, Ron McMillan, Al Switzler, and David Maxfield
  - *How Did That Happen? Holding People Accountable for Results the Positive, Principled Way* by Roger Connors and Tom Smith

Dedicate at least 30 minutes a week to reading these resources. For a period of 60 days, make note of the things you learn and new things you would like to try. Review these with your manager or a trusted peer. Discuss how you can incorporate these learnings into your routine.

Ideas for leveraging:

- **Coach people who avoid accountability.** Act as a personal mentor for people who lack the courage to own up to their mistakes, or the confidence to stand by their decisions. Help them understand how you acknowledge your own mistakes, and most of all how you learn from them. Give them specific examples of the accomplishments you're most proud of and the failures you've had to cope with. Then help them address their own situations, coaching them on how to admit defeat *and* accept praise graciously. Meet with them throughout the process to review their thoughts and concerns. Keep track of your activities and learnings in this area.

- **Model personal accountability.** Create case studies of times that you've had to defend your decisions and admit your mistakes. How did you prepare yourself? How did you overcome your fears? What obstacles did you encounter? What were the results? Document these examples, and find a way to share them with people, either through casual lunch-n-learns or one-on-one coaching.

- **Conduct one-on-one or small group training sessions about personal accountability.** Topics may include:
  - Learning to admit to your mistakes
  - Sharing case scenarios with "lessons learned" from previous organizational/departmental projects
  - Planning ahead and being proactive to increase your chances for success

- **Host a virtual or live lunch-n-learn to discuss the importance of accountability.** Prepare a discussion around the importance of being proactive and accountable. Discuss common issues that get in the way of taking responsibility, such as fear of failure, lack of confidence, or being defensive. Use past examples from times you owned up to your own mistakes, how you felt, and how others reacted. Keep track of the work you do and the impact it has on others.

Behavior 3: Exhibits Intellectual Curiosity

What would you like to learn more about right now? Have you sought out ways to learn more? People who exhibit intellectual curiosity are relentless and versatile learners. They collect information from a wide range of sources and make connections among previously unrelated notions. They enjoy the challenge of unfamiliar tasks and ask meaningful questions. They are personally committed to continuous learning.

Ideas for improving this skill:

- **Increase your knowledge of unfamiliar subjects.** Pay attention to trends and ideas in different areas, such as art, science, pop culture, and business. Expose yourself to new thinking, even when it seems that ideas do not apply to your life. Try this: For the next month, read one blog post or article, or watch a video or presentation, from a new source every day. Choose sources that are outside of your regular comfort zone. For example, if you listen to rock music, read about a famous jazz musician. If you don't know a thing about modern art, check out the Museum of Modern Art. The point is to open up your mind to new and different ideas. Keep track of what you learn about each day in a journal. At the end of the month, review what you've learned. Which ideas or information impressed you the most? Did you learn anything that sparks a new idea? Make note of your observations, and share them with your manager or a friend.

- **Expand your network to include a diverse group of people.** When your personal interactions represent many different viewpoints, your thoughts and assumptions will regularly be challenged. Evaluate your network with a critical eye: How diverse is it? What gaps exist? How many people in your network typically have views different from your own? Push yourself to grow the diversity of your network. Look across industries, socio-economic backgrounds, ages, and pay-grade to find people who can offer unique insight and new ways of thinking through things. When you meet new people, strike up a conversation to learn about their interests or line of work.

Send LinkedIn messages or invitations to connect to interesting people, and talk with them over coffee. As you ask them about themselves, think about how their approaches or ideas could possibly be applied to your life or work. Track your efforts over the next 30 days and then share your learnings with your manager or a trusted peer.

- **Build a library of great thoughts.** Over the next three months, ask people to send you great work: presentations, whitepapers, videos, or articles. Ask for work that describes interesting thought models or approaches, good graphics that explain a "current state" or new idea, or provocative articles, videos, or quotations. The age of the document or the discipline from which the presentation comes doesn't matter. Read these articles as they come in, and think about ways they could be adapted to your experience. What can you learn from the ideas or problems presented? Make notes of your discoveries. At the end of the three months, review your library with your manager or a friend, and share the top three things you learned.

- **Deliberately seek out different opinions and perspectives.** Make a list of people you know who tend to have different perspectives from you. This may include people with opposite political leanings, people who favor the other one-half of the brain (right-brained versus left-brained), or people from different countries or cultural backgrounds. Schedule a lunch or coffee with these people once a month for the next three months. During these exchanges, do everything you can to understand how they see different situations. Topics can vary, from a new TV show to a specific news story. Do not use this time to debate their point of view, but simply to understand it. Ask them questions such as How did you reach that conclusion? or Why do you feel that way? After each conversation, make notes in your plan about what you learned and what surprised you. Have your assumptions about these people changed? What has this experience taught you about perception versus reality?

- **Give your brain a workout.** Exercising your brain can increase your knowledge *and* your curiosity. For the next 8 weeks, make a concerted effort to do one of these tasks at least twice a week:

- ○ Read the science or technology section of the newspaper or news website.

- ○ Solve a tough puzzle.

- ○ Engage in thoughtful arguments.

- ○ Talk with intelligent people about a meaty topic.

- ○ Track your efforts in this area in your plan, and note points that you thought were interesting, what was fun or engaging about the activity, or even how you might apply what you learned. After 60 days, you should have at least 16 tasks on your list. Reflect on what you've learned and applied. Did you share an article with someone? Persuade others to share your point of view? Learn about or apply a new model of thinking? Share your process and learnings with your manager or a trusted advisor.

- **Learn to ask "why" more often.** The next time you are faced with an issue, or discover something that surprises you, don't just accept it at face value. Learn to ask "why." This little word will do more to expand your thinking than any big complicated idea. When you are requested to do something, or you receive some feedback, or someone expresses an opinion different from your own, ask for the thinking behind it. Then dig deeper to discover the "whys" behind that. For example: Your manager asks you to re-analyze some data. Why? Because her manager thinks there was an error. Why? Because she wasn't happy with what the data told her. Why? Because it contradicts a promise she already made to someone else. Now you know that the problem probably isn't the data, but the story the data tells. With this knowledge, you can frame the data in a different way that will help the real problem. For the next two weeks, keep a list of all the "whys" you ask, and what you discover. At the end of the two weeks, see if you can draw any conclusions. Make note of what you would never have known if you hadn't asked "why?" and how that lack of knowledge would have affected you. Share your key findings with your manager or a friend.

- **Read books that inspire innovative and creative problem solving strategies.** Suggestions include:
  - *Questions That Work: How to Ask Questions That Will Help You Succeed in Any Business Situation* by Andrew Finlayson
  - *Thinking, Fast and Slow* by Daniel Kahneman
  - *Problem Solving 101: A Simple Book for Smart People* by Ken Watanabe

  Dedicate at least 30 minutes per week to reading. For a period of 60 days, make note of the things you learn and new things you'd like to try. Review these with a trusted peer or your manager. Discuss how you can incorporate these learnings into your routine.

Ideas for leveraging:

- **Coach people who are seeking to develop their intellectual curiosity.** Review your approach to solving problems and thinking through issues. Share with them the top five resources you use (blogs, websites, columnists, video interviews, and more) to challenge your own thinking and how often you refer to them. Learn about their approaches to learning; then help them determine their biggest areas of opportunity, and suggest your ideas for improvement. Coach them through a creative process and share your thinking and feedback regularly. Identify places in which they could have been more curious and gathered more information and opinions to inform their results. Offer to role-play with this person, debating a topic to open up their thinking and expand their perspective. Meet with them throughout the process to review their thoughts and concerns. Keep track of your activities and learnings in this area.

- **Develop a short presentation reviewing your approach to continuous learning.** Include tips, best practices, resources and real-world examples and cases to showcase your experience and knowledge. Host a virtual or in-person training session with people who want to improve in this area. As an alternative, share your presentation online: Film a short video and post it on YouTube, or create a PowerPoint presentation and post it on your own blog, or on another platform. Keep track of your work in this area and share your learnings with your manager.

- **Create a list of your "go-to" information resources.** Create different categories of information, such as Industry, Business, Technology, Science, and Politics. Under each category, list reliable resources that you find provocative, challenging, and applicable to your life or work. Include different types of media and formats, such as blogs, websites, columnists, video interviews, motivational talks, music videos, and magazines. Publish this resource list in the best ways and spread the word about it. Ask for others' contributions as well.

- **Offer to play the "devil's advocate" role.** Become the person others can turn to when they need to check their logic or ideas. Challenge them by asking questions such as: Where did you get your information? Who did you talk to? What are your resources? Is there a different way of looking at this problem? Help others learn to step up their own intellectual curiosity by demonstrating your own. Over time, track your efforts in this area and the outcomes you believe they lead to. Consider the best approach for playing the "devil's advocate" in the most productive way. Share your learnings with your manager or a friend.

Behavior 4: Develops Self

What does it mean to develop yourself? People who develop themselves learn quickly when facing new problems. They are open to criticism and feedback. They gain insights from mistakes and are constantly looking for, and taking, opportunities to learn new skills and improve existing ones.

Ideas for improving this skill:

- **Learn about yourself.** Seek out self-assessment tools such as the Enneagram, Meyers-Briggs, and DiSC or free online tools (search "free assessments"). Through a series of questions, tools such as these can help you discover your natural strengths and challenges, and give you helpful ideas for development.

Commit to using at least one self-assessment tool within the next 30 days. Make notes about what you learn, and think about what rings true. Share your findings with your manager or a friend and ask for their opinion.

- **Actively seek feedback.** Within the next 30 days, choose a few people who work with you regularly who you trust. Set up time to ask for their honest feedback about your skills and behaviors. Questions to ask them include:
  - What do I do best?
  - When am I at my best (for example, speaking in front of large groups, small group meetings, or interactions; connecting people with similar interests or goals, and so on)?
  - Where are my greatest areas for improvement?
  - What interpersonal skills should I focus on improving?
  - Can you give me an example of when I've excelled? How about an example of a something I could have handled better?

  Beforehand, prepare yourself to hear both the positives and negatives, and practice graciously accepting compliments and critiques. Avoid seeking feedback when you are tired or emotionally drained. At the end of the session, let them know you appreciate their candor.

  Make notes about what you learned during this process. Identify at least one skill you want to focus on as a result, and share your insights with your manager or a trusted advisor.

- **Find a role model.** Within the next 30 days, choose a peer who you consider to be perceptive and self-aware. Take her to lunch and quiz her about her practices for self-development. What structures does she have in place to access feedback from others? How does she handle criticism? How does she use what she hears to improve her performance? Take notes and consider how you might use her tips to build your own self-development plan. Share your findings and plans with your manager or a mentor.

- **Learn how to accept criticism.** Any type of feedback, especially constructive criticism, is essential to your development.

If you become defensive or shut down when others give you feedback, people will be reluctant to approach you and you'll lose a valuable opportunity to learn about yourself. For the next 30 days, try changing your attitude about feedback. Instead of hearing feedback as a personal attack, listen for the lessons in the comments. Take deep breaths, don't interrupt, maintain eye contact, and avoid offering explanations, which can sound defensive. Finally, thank the person for sharing their insights. Keep notes about what you learn and how you feel during this process. Share your insights with your manager or a trusted friend.

- **Utilize project look-backs.** At the end of each project you are involved with over the next 60 days, analyze what went well and what could have been done more efficiently or effectively, and celebrate successes. Ask for feedback from others specifically about your own performance as well. Identify at least one key learning you can apply to your next project. Share your insights with your manager or a peer.

- **Keep a journal and learn from every situation.** Even negative or challenging experiences are worthwhile if you learn something from them. Over the next 60 days, take initiative to respond constructively to challenges, and make note of your actions, reactions, and insights. Talk to your manager or peers to gain their perspective as well. Make notes on what you learn about yourself during this process. Were you able to apply learnings from one situation to another? What were the top two most valuable learnings? How can you make sure you remember them? Share your insights with your manager or an advisor.

- **Stay well informed about new approaches and techniques.** Attend professional networking events, listen to presentations, and read leadership and development magazines and blogs for new ideas to inspire you. Join a LinkedIn group and exchange ideas with colleagues in other companies. Some good resources include Smartbrief on Leadership and Leadership Excellence. Commit to aggressive learning for the next 60 days and keep track of the new knowledge and ideas you pick up, and be sure to share them with your manager or a mentor.

- **Look for patterns.** Over the next 30 days, review your successes and your failures from the last year. What are the commonalities between them? Consider your language, the setting, particular personalities, and the issue involved. What can you learn from these experiences? What familiar approaches can you build on? Make notes of potential causes and effects. How you can duplicate the successes? How can you alter your actions for a different outcome? Make notes of the patterns you notice and what they are telling you. Share your insights with your manager or a friend.

- **Build awareness around how you like to receive feedback.** Think about instances in which you've received feedback in the past. Identify and record the instances in which the feedback was well received and led to positive change and growth. When did it go well? Why? When did it not go well? Why? Think about circumstances and factors associated with these situations and record them. Ask yourself questions like, How do I like to receive feedback? What settings work best for me? What advice would I give to the person offering me feedback? After you have made this list, share it with people who are likely to give you constructive feedback. Put this approach into action for the next 90 days. Later, share your learnings and outcomes with your manager or an advisor.

- **Create a development goal.** Identify a new skill, knowledge, or experience that you want to attain and put a plan together to achieve that goal. As you put your plan together, think about the following:

  o What do you want to accomplish? (Identify specific, measureable, attainable, realistic, and timely goals.)

  o Where are you today in relation to this goal and how do you need to fill the gap?

  o What can you do to close these gaps? (For example, brainstorm a full range of options and decide on a few.)

  o What will you do to accomplish your goal and when will you accomplish it?

  If you do not already have one, create a formal development plan to define your goal, the actions you will take, and the timelines for when you will complete it. Share this plan with a mentor and keep track of your progress. Measure your success on the progress you make toward reaching your goal. Use the document to facilitate a conversation about development with your manager or a friend.

- **Read books that inspire self-improvement.** Suggestions include:
  - *The Power of Habit: Why We Do What We Do in Life and Business* by Charles Duhigg
  - *Self-Improvement 101: What Every Leader Needs to Know* by John C. Maxwell
  - *The 7 Habits of Highly Effective People: Powerful Lessons in Personal Change* by Stephen Covey
  - *Playing Big: Find Your Voice, Your Mission, Your Message* by Tara Mohr

Dedicate at least 30 minutes a week to reading these resources. For a period of 60 days, make note of the things you learn and new things you would like to try. Review these with your manager or a trusted peer. Discuss how you can incorporate these learnings into your routine.

Ideas for leveraging:

- **Coach people who do not regularly practice self-development.** Identify their hesitation. Do they lack confidence? Do they think they are "as good as it gets"? Are they afraid of feedback? Help them face their fears by sharing your real-life examples and situations. Coach them as they choose a plan to identify their areas for improvement. Help them determine the best methods for learning new skills. Meet with them throughout the process to review their thoughts and concerns. Keep track of your activities and learnings in this area.

- **Share your personal self-improvement methods.** Create case studies of times that you've needed to change your own approach to something. How did you know you needed to make an adjustment? How did you respond? What were the results? Document these examples, and find a way to share them with people, either through casual lunch-n-learns or one-on-one coaching.

- **Develop a short presentation that helps others learn to learn.** Include tips, best practices, resources, and real-world examples around topics such as how to gather feedback, how to receive criticism graciously, and how to apply feedback to development plans. Review the most common obstacles to self-development and how to overcome them. Host a virtual or in-person training session with people who want to improve in this area. As an alternative, share your presentation online: shoot a short video and post it on YouTube, or create a PowerPoint presentation and post it on your own blog or on another platform.

- **Build a best-practice guide for self-development.** Include methods you have used successfully, as well as ideas from peers and colleagues outside your organization (see Figure 6.1). Include templates for feedback questions and development plans, as well as online learning resources. Put the guide into different formats that can be easily accessed by others: paper copies, blog postings, or in a group sharing platform. Keep track of the work you do and the impact it seems to have on others.

Figure 6.1 Self-directed development: what's in it for each group

7

Development Library for Leaders

Behavior 1: Challenges Norms Appropriately

Behavior 2: Manages Courageously

Behavior 3: Navigates Ambiguity

Behavior 4: Creates a Culture of Innovation

Behavior 5: Motivates Others

Behavior 6: Selects Talent

Behavior 7: Develops Others

Introduction

The purpose of this chapter is to describe behaviors for leaders who want to improve the way learning and development takes place in the organization.

Behavior 1: Challenges Norms Appropriately

Think back to a time when you stood up for something you knew was right, even if those around you didn't agree. People who challenge norms appropriately demonstrate the courage and initiative to speak up when encountering something that doesn't seem right or when they have a strong conviction. They ask questions assertively and respectfully and thoughtfully question both their own and others' assumptions. They develop a solid case for change and present alternative solutions without undermining other leaders. They can still "fall in line" and show support if their proposed alternatives are not approved.

Ideas for improving this skill:

- **If you tend to be too aggressive with your opinions, learn when—and how—to deliver your opposing view.** To pitch your ideas successfully, look for the right opportunity and present them in the right way. If you tend to be too aggressive with your opinions, try this approach:

  ○ *Find the right time and place.* There are times when you may not want to express an opposing view in a public forum or in front of your team. Be sure to consider all the consequences of what you're saying: Will it undermine another leader? Is it a highly emotional subject? Is there some confidential information behind the other argument that can't be shared in a broader forum? Think through these issues to determine the best time for the conversation.

  ○ *Learn to read your audience.* If they are nodding and appear interested, you have made a connection. If they are distracted, checking their cell phones or seeming impatient, chances are they aren't agreeing with you or understanding you. Pick up on the signals and continue or end your pitch accordingly.

  Over the next 60 days, think through these points before you pitch new ideas or challenge any existing programs and policies. Sketch out your arguments and determine where, when, and with whom you should share them. Practice your delivery on video and in front of a trusted peer, and monitor your tone and language. Keep track of what you do, and share your insights with your manager or an advisor.

- **If you tend to be too understated in your opinions, learn to articulate your arguments with passion.** When you pitch a new solution to a problem, it's imperative that you communicate with passion. If you struggle to get your point across in a manner that conveys conviction and the depth of your commitment, try this step-by-step approach for the next 30 to 60 days.

  First, plan *what* you'll say. Before you enter a discussion, be clear on your point of view and why. Determine beforehand what impact you want to make. Plan for the questions and objections that your audience may have.

Second, practice *how* you'll say it. Ask a friend to record you on video as you state your point of view. Watch yourself to see if you:

o Dilute your comments with phrases such as "Don't you think?" and "Can I ask you?"

o Speak in a succinct and direct way.

o Look at your audience in the eye.

o Convey conviction when you explain your point of view.

Make note of what you need to work on. Keep track of what you learn throughout this process, and watch how you improve each time you practice. Share your progress with your manager or a trusted peer.

- **Analyze and face any fears you have of visibly taking a stand.** First, if you are regularly uneasy or reluctant to take a stand, try to identify why that is. Are you afraid of being disliked? Does potential conflict make you uncomfortable? Are you concerned about being reprimanded? Within the next 30 days, document the reasons behind your hesitation. Share your list with a trusted peer or mentor, and ask for their ideas about overcoming your fears. Seek out examples of others who have spoken up, with success or not. What can you learn from these real-life examples? Begin to plan for those occasions when you feel unsure of yourself. What small steps can you commit to so that you can build your confidence? Share your insights with your manager or a friend.

- **If you'd like to be more assertive, create opportunities to practice.** Try three or more of these techniques for 30 days and track your progress:

o Find a coach or role model who can help you learn to be more assertive.

o Observe and study how assertive people start discussions, deal with interruptions, express their views, and respond to criticism.

o Practice clearly stating your point of view directly and confidently, especially when you are in safe environments, interacting with those close to you.

○ Pay attention to how you feel when you ask for what you want. Note the difference in how other people treat you when you are assertive. Use these reflections to motivate you to continue to assert yourself.

○ Say no when you need to; don't procrastinate or appear tentative. Monitor your nonverbal actions to make sure they are in alignment with your words (for example, make eye contact and stand up straight).

Keep track of the instances in which you put these approaches into action, both within and outside of work. Make note of your learnings and the outcomes. Later, share this information with your manager or a mentor and recognize your progress.

- **Research those industry giants who inspire possibilities.** Over the next 30 days, identify three people from various industries who are known for spearheading new ideas and creating new possibilities for others. Study the techniques they used to identify their ideas and how they aligned with others to make their visions a reality. Pay attention to behaviors they used to inspire those around them and to drive themselves forward even when faced with adversity. How did they move from an idea to implementation? Record key techniques you would like to work on in your own department or area. Share your learnings and outcomes with your manager or a trusted advisor.

- **Question whether processes should be improved, eliminated, or disrupted.** Before moving too quickly to improve or adjust a process or tool, take time to challenge the basic assumptions of what is being done. What are the purpose and the outcome of the current process? Is the outcome useful or valuable? Does it make sense to make the process more efficient or improve it in some way? Or is it actually better to eliminate it because it is not adding value to the business? Apply this approach with a potential project or initiative within the next 60 days. Reflect on what you have learned as you've challenged basic assumptions, and share how you will apply these learnings with your manager or a friend.

- **Encourage those around you to rigorously examine the current state of reality.** As a leader, foster a climate in which all team members diligently get to the truth and allow each other to be heard. When a problem arises, ask "why" and "why" again until you gain understanding, and avoid using discussions as a process to assign blame. Leverage questions such as, "What's on your mind?" "Can you help me to understand about...?" And "What should we be worried or concerned about?" On a daily basis, stop and reflect. Ask yourself how many times you started a conversation with a question. Did you obtain a clear and honest picture of the current state? Did you sense that anyone was "sugar-coating" the information? If so, in what area? How did you give others permission to be honest with their feedback? Did the group come to the best answer or was the answer predetermined? Evaluate yourself and consider what things you can continue to do to build a climate of rigorous examination. Put this approach into action for the next 90 days. Afterward, reflect on how it has impacted your team's ability to raise standards and move beyond automatic assumptions about the current state. Later, share your learnings and outcomes with your manager or a trusted advisor.

- **Build your ability to challenge an existing norm by starting small.** Identify a real but low-risk need and create a better solution. Within the next 30-60 days, choose a process or program that doesn't work well for you. Break down the process into individual steps to identify exactly what and where the problems are. Then create a few different scenarios to resolve these issues. (These may involve changing prescribed roles, adjusting timelines, eliminating steps, and so on.) Review your ideas with your manager, and note where you receive pushback. Take time to process what you learned during this exercise and how you can apply these learnings to bigger, more visible changes you'd like to propose.

- **Identify an improvement and change that you would like to implement, and build a case for it.** Over the next 30 days, follow these steps:

1. Identify the 5 W's related to your idea. (Why does it matter? Why is it important? Who is involved? What are possible results? Where and when will the change take place? How will this improvement help our organization?)

2. Complete a high-level stakeholder analysis. (Who will be impacted; how they might respond, and so on.)

3. Create a formal presentation and share your findings with your manager or team.

4. Solicit input and feedback following your presentation. Probe to determine how you could have been even more effective, including information about what, if anything, you failed to consider.

Keep a list of the things and ideas you plan on incorporating into your approach going forward. Share your learnings with your manager or a trusted peer.

- **Identify an internal role model who consistently implements change with success.** Choose someone in your organization who has challenged "the way it's always been done" and proposed a better process or product. Within the next 30 to 60 days, partner with him to evaluate the behaviors and approaches he used. Ask him to explain how he shed light on the issue and proposed different solutions, while maintaining appropriate respect for leadership. Ask him to walk through the business case for change and how it was built. Review the data he presented and how he decided what to include and not to include. Discuss examples of how he took his belief to idea to plan to implementation. Explore how he gained support from various levels of management in the organization. See if he would be willing to provide feedback to you regarding progress on a change you are currently implementing. Jot down what you are learning and commit to implementing at least one major idea in the next 60 days. Share your learnings and outcomes with your manager or an advisor.

- **Learn to understand, anticipate, and work with resistance.** Resistance to change can sabotage the most well-planned strategy. Think of a change you have faced at work that was unexpected and perhaps unwanted. Consider how the people around you responded, and what leaders did as a result. What behaviors did they engage in? Did their actions or responses illicit more or less resistance? Learn from the leaders who led the change successfully. Chances are they:

- Communicated why the change was important, in language that resonated with their stakeholders and employees

- Responded appropriately to the "rumor mill" by intentionally seeking out information and immediately sharing the facts

- Minimized fear by creating and implementing activities that built new skills and abilities

- Allowed their team enough time to adjust to change, and were patient while they navigated the learning curve

Continue to observe as leaders introduce new ideas and process improvements. Make note about their successes, as well as when their efforts fall short. Identify at least three things you will try to do to both anticipate and work with resistance in a healthy way the next time you propose an idea for change. Share what you are learning with your manager or a colleague.

- **Learn to "lose" with composure.** It can be difficult to accept that an idea you believe in will not be approved or implemented by your organization. However, as a leader it is crucial that you can process the "defeat" and still visibly support your organization's stance—even when you don't agree with it. If you struggle in this area, try these tips:

  - *Express your disappointment/displeasure in a nonwork setting.* Do your venting at home or with friends outside of the organization.

  - *Write down your thoughts and feelings in a private journal.*

  - *Remain positive with your team.* Although you can admit that things didn't go the way you had proposed, show your support for the outcome. Point out the positive effects ("Now we won't have to spend time creating new documentation," "The consistency is important," and so on), and then move on.

- o Commit to these steps the next time you face disappointment. Share your insights with your manager or a friend.
- **Read books that detail effective ways to challenge the norm and orchestrate change.** Suggestions include:
  - o *First, Break All the Rules: What the World's Greatest Managers Do Differently* by Marcus Buckingham and Curt Coffman
  - o *Leading Change* by John P. Kotter
  - o *Making Strategy Work: Leading Effective Execution and Change* by Lawrence Hrebiniak
  - o *Do More Great Work: Stop the Busywork. Start the Work That Matters* by Michael Bungay Stanier and Seth Godin
  - o *The Power of Business Process Improvement: 10 Simple Steps to Increase Effectiveness, Efficiency, and Adaptability* by Susan Page

  Dedicate at least 30 minutes a week to reading these resources. For a period of 60 days, make note of the things you learn and new things you would like to try. Review these with your manager and a trusted peer. Discuss how you can incorporate these learnings into your routine.

Ideas for leveraging:

- **Coach people who seek increased confidence in speaking up.** Learn about their fears, help them determine their biggest areas of opportunity, and suggest your ideas for improvement. Review your approach to challenging "the way it's always been done" while maintaining respect for other leaders. Observe them in interactions with others, and identify places where they could be more persuasive. Meet with them throughout the process to review their thoughts and concerns. Keep track of your activities and learnings in this area. Assess how effectively you coach and the outcome of progress made. Share your activities and learnings with your manager or a trusted peer over time.

- **Conduct one-on-one or small group training sessions about building a business case for your idea for change.** Ideas include:
  - Elements of building a persuasive case for change
  - Anticipating and planning for resistance
  - Expressing your point of view with passion but not inflexibility
  - Evaluation of types of data to include and the best way to convey and present them.

  Keep track of the work you do and the impact it seems to have on others. Share your activity and learnings with your manager or a trusted advisor.

- **Develop a short presentation reviewing your methods of leading change that disrupts the status quo for people.** Include tips, best practices, resources, and real-world examples and cases to showcase your experience and knowledge. Topics may include:
  - How to be respectful of the norms while proposing changes to them
  - Creating opportunities for input
  - Developing a clear communication plan
  - Guiding ideas all the way through implementation
  - Accepting a "loss" and moving on

  Host a virtual or in-person training session with people who want to improve in this area. As an alternative, share your presentation online: Shoot a short video and post it on YouTube, or create a PowerPoint presentation and post it on your own blog, or on SlideShare. Keep track of your work in this area and share your learnings with your manager or a trusted peer.

- **Build a best-practice guide for how to successfully propose and shepherd ideas through your organization.** Include methods you have used successfully, as well as ideas from peers and colleagues outside your organization. Put the guide into different formats that can be easily accessed by others: paper copies, blog postings, and in a group sharing platform.

Keep track of the work you do and the impact it seems to have on others. Share your activity and learnings with your manager or a peer.

Behavior 2: Manages Courageously

Leaders who manage courageously are open and forthright without being perceived as threatening. They deal with problems (people-related or other) fairly and firmly and in a timely manner. They act with the view of what is best for their organization long term. They don't hold back on anything that needs to be said and say it respectfully so others can hear it. They aren't afraid to take negative action when necessary and shoulder responsibility for their own and team decisions.

Ideas for improving this skill:

- **Clarify and affirm your leadership role in your own mind.** If you struggle to make tough calls with the people you lead, ask yourself if you are afraid of being unpopular. Remember, as a leader your responsibility is to help your people perform to their best ability—not to be their friend. Although good managers can be friendly and should be approachable, these traits should not get in the way of delivering tough feedback. To assess if this is a problem for you, within the next 30 days, ask for candid feedback from a fellow manager whom you trust. Listen carefully to her response and take notes. Commit to one thing you will do differently to build your confidence and reputation as a leader. Make note of the changes you put into practice and pay attention to how others respond. Review your learnings and your plan with your manager or a trusted advisor.

- **Communicate clear standards to your people.** Make sure your people know exactly what is expected of them. Within the next 30 days, meet with each of your team members and review their key responsibilities and what they will be held accountable for. Put these expectations in writing, and give a copy to your employees. After you set this baseline, it is easier to point out how they are making meaningful contributions and where improvements need to be made in the future. Review the documents with your manager or a trusted colleague and get their feedback.

- **Learn how to better prepare yourself for performance discussions.** Before you confront someone with tough feedback, take some time to think through your approach. Use these guidelines:

  ○ Keep your list to just one or two feedback points.

  ○ Provide specific examples of when people have not met your expectations.

  ○ Ask for their thoughts and pay attention to their reactions.

  ○ Explain what you want to see them do differently, and reinforce your expectations.

  Write down your thoughts and run through them a few times before the conversation. Try this more structured approach for the next 60 days, and note the outcomes of these conversations...has performance improved? Track the results of these conversations. Share your learnings and progress with your manager or a peer.

- **Practice delivering difficult feedback.** The best way to improve your ability to give tough feedback is to practice. Your goal is to be clear, confident, unemotional, and yet approachable. Over the next 30 to 60 days, ask a peer to practice with you, playing the role of the employee receiving your feedback. After you're done, ask your partner: Was the feedback communicated clearly? Did I explain what behavior needs to change in the future? Did I maintain eye contact? A calm tone of voice? Open body language? Did I give the employee time to ask questions? Keep practicing until you feel more confident. Although you will probably never enjoy having tough conversations, they will always be part of your job as a leader—and you can become more comfortable facilitating them. Keep track of your progress and share your insights with your manager or an advisor.

- **Allow adequate time for others to demonstrate development.** Remember that it takes time to develop a new skill or change behaviors. Don't expect to see an immediate turnaround after you deliver tough feedback. Set a challenging, yet fair, timeline for improvement, and give appropriate support and feedback along the way. Let your people know that you want them to succeed. Implement this thinking into your leadership philosophy over the next 60 to 90 days. Note how having realistic expectations reduces your level of frustration and empowers your people. Share your insights with your manager or a mentor.

- **Learn to create effective performance plans.** When someone on your team is consistently performing below standards, it may be time to create a more formal performance plan. Ask someone from your HR team to give you an overview of what specific actions and policies should be followed when creating a performance improvement plan. Good performance plans include:

  o Specific examples of discrepancies between the expectations and the performance

  o An agreement on what the employee will do differently

  o Specific check-in points and deadlines

  Over the next 30 to 60 days, initiate performance plans when necessary. Keep track of the steps you take, discussions you have, your key observations, and learnings. Review them with your manager and a trusted advisor.

- **Find a mentor who displays managerial courage.** Within the next 30 days, identify someone who makes tough calls when necessary. Ask to have coffee with this person, and talk about the challenges she has encountered and how she dealt with them. Ask how she delivers tough feedback and manages performance, and if she would consider sharing a performance plan with you (anonymously). Make notes of what you learn, and choose a few techniques to try with your own people. Share your insights with your manager or a peer.

- **Read books that inspire courageous leadership.** Suggestions include:

  ○ *Courageous Visions: How to Unleash Passionate Energy in Your Life and Your Organization* by Martha Lasley

  ○ *Courage: The Backbone of Leadership* by Gus Lee and Diane Elliott-Lee

  ○ *Find Your Courage: 12 Acts for Becoming Fearless at Work and in Life* by Margie Warrell

  Dedicate at least 30 minutes a week to reading these resources. For a period of 60 days, make note of the things you learn and new things you would like to try. Review these with your manager and a trusted peer. Discuss how you can incorporate these learnings into your routine.

Ideas for leveraging:

- **Coach other leaders who avoid addressing problems with their employees.** Offer to help them prepare for tough conversations and then role-play with them. Help them find different approaches to specific situations that are challenging them. Encourage them to commit to making two or three changes to build their managerial courage. Check in with them afterward to see how they're doing. Give them feedback based on what you observe. Keep track of your activities and observations in this area, as well as feedback from the people you coach, and share them with your manager or an advisor.

- **Participate in "tough conversation" role-plays.** Pair up with someone who struggles to deliver tough feedback. Play the role of the employee, allowing your partner to practice leading the conversation. Give him feedback about what he did well and how he can improve. Demonstrate how you would approach the same conversation. Keep track of your activities in this area, as well as feedback from the person you're coaching, and share them with your manager or a trusted friend.

- **Develop a workshop about best practices in managerial courage.** Agenda items could include:
  - Preparing for tough conversations
  - The benefits of role-playing as part of your preparation
  - How to remain calm and focused even when others are upset
  - Creating a performance plan to improve a direct report's performance
  - The line between manager and friend

  Host a virtual or in-person training session with people who want to improve in this area. As an alternative, share your presentation online: Shoot a short video and post it on YouTube, or create a PowerPoint presentation and post it on your own blog or on SlideShare. Keep track of your activities in this area—and the feedback from your attendees—and share it with your manager or a peer.

- **Partner with Human Resources and share your examples of working through difficult performance issues with others.** Document your approach, templates, and "scripts" for conducting performance plans. Be sure to keep the templates anonymous; remove any names or information that would reveal the person who actually received the plan. Include an FAQ section. Find a partner in HR to share these templates and best practices, either through a department meeting, a blog, or by speaking at other groups' events. Review your plans and progress with your manager or an advisor.

Behavior 3: Navigates Ambiguity

Sometimes, it's not possible to have the information or clarity we would like to have to make a decision. Leaders who navigate ambiguity can comfortably handle uncertainty. They can move forward without complete information and can shift gears with ease. They aren't upset when issues are unresolved in spite of everyone's best efforts. They are adaptable to change and help lead others through change.

Ideas for improving this skill:

- **Focus on finding the opportunity in ambiguity.** When you're going through change, it can feel like you're swimming in a sea of ambiguity. You might ask, "How will things work now?" or "What will this mean for me?" The great part about ambiguity is that you can forge your own ways of working. Try this: Consider a change you are facing within the next 60 days. Where processes or procedures aren't clear, take the lead in designing approaches that reflect your interests and goals. Share your plans and ideas with your manager or a mentor.

- **Expect the unexpected, and prepare accordingly.** Over the next 30 days, consider a work assignment or project you're starting, and brainstorm alternative approaches to it, given different unexpected constraints. Brainstorm ways that you would modify your approach to the project in a scenario in which you had fewer participants than expected. Or less money. Or a tighter deadline. Or broader scope. Thinking of options can help you be prepared if you have to shift gears in short order. Share your thoughts on this process—and your alternative approaches—with your manager or a trusted advisor, and discuss other situations in which multiple options are frequently needed.

- **Learn from the past experiences of others, and apply those learnings to your situation.** By learning from the experiences of others, we can better predict (or at least prepare for) shifts that might occur. Over the next 60 days, poll each of your trusted colleagues to learn about their experiences when work efforts, presentations, or projects have had to shift course quickly. For the examples that they provide, list the cause and the response. Look for patterns. Is the shift typically due to changing business conditions? A new stakeholder on the scene? A customer trend? How did your colleagues respond to these shifts? What was successful? What did they learn? Would they have done anything different in retrospect? Review your analysis with your manager or a trusted peer, and talk about how you might apply your learnings right away.

- **Build a thriving network that can help you through times of change or uncertainty.** Your ability to adapt can depend upon the breadth of your network that you rely on to obtain timely news, tap subject matter experts, and gain support for your ideas. Over the next 30 days, examine your network of colleagues, and build a plan to nurture it: See where there are gaps in expertise, and plan to meet someone who can fill the gap. Send a note of greetings to previous contacts to keep them close. When you face a situation in which you must quickly change directions, consider communicating with those in your network to gain information and insights, knowledge, and support. Share your network plan with your manager or a peer, and ask for feedback on new ways or areas to build relationships. Ask whether they can suggest any of their contacts for you to meet. Track your progress, and circle back with your manager or peer regularly.

- **Find a mentor who has thrived despite ambiguity.** Identify someone who made it through uncertainty and change, and was more successful as a result. Ask them to give you examples of how their jobs, plans, and projects changed midstream, and how they handled the uncertainty. Learn about their approach to change and how they respond to shifts in direction or new situations. Lean on them during the shifts you face, and approach them with your questions and concerns. Over the next 60 to 90 days, keep track of your work in this area, and share your learnings with your manager or a trusted friend.

- **Take on a problem with no clear solution.** Within the next 30 to 60 days, ask a peer or your manager to identify an issue that is "fuzzy," with no clear steps or outcome. Offer to help explore and navigate the issue. Learn whatever you can about the circumstances, facts, and people who are involved. Note where the ambiguity is coming from: Are there conflicting opinions from leaders? Are the roles too loosely defined? Meet with your manager and propose a few different approaches to help resolve the issue. Ask for feedback, and keep track of what you learn and can apply to your next issue.

- **Reflect upon past times of ambiguity and capture your learnings to apply going forward.** Over the next 30 days, take time to remember past situations in which you faced uncertainty. Perhaps a leader changed strategy midstream, or you were told you might lose funding for a project. Journal about your experiences, and reflect upon how you felt throughout the process. When did you feel most uncomfortable? When did you start feeling better? How did you cope (or not cope) with the ambiguity? What was the outcome? What did you learn from the experience? Make notes of the themes and concepts that resonate the most with you, and keep a list of the things and ideas you plan on incorporating into your approach going forward. Share your learnings with your manager or an advisor.

- **When dealing with limited information, map out the best-case/worst-case scenarios.** The next time you must take action with only limited information, look at both sides of the decision (that is, "go" or "no-go"). For each side, write down the best-case scenario and the worst-case scenario given the information you have. Compare the scenarios. Does any scenario seem far too risky? Does any scenario have limited upside? Put this approach into action when analyzing ambiguous situations for the next 60 days. Later, share your learnings and outcomes with your manager or a trusted mentor.

- **Read books that provide insight on effectively navigating ambiguity.** Suggestions include:
  - *Switch: How to Change Things When Change Is Hard* by Chip Heath and Dan Heath
  - *Who Moved My Cheese?: An Amazing Way to Deal with Change in Your Work and in Your Life* by Spencer Johnson and Kenneth Blanchard
  - *Adaptability: The Art of Winning in an Age of Uncertainty* by Max McKeown
  - *Great by Choice: Uncertainty, Chaos, and Luck—Why Some Thrive Despite Them All* by Jim Collins and Morten T. Hansen

Dedicate at least 30 minutes a week to reading these resources. For a period of 60 days, make note of the things you learn and new things you would like to try. Review these with your manager and a trusted peer. Discuss how you can incorporate these learnings into your routine.

Ideas for leveraging:

- **Coach people who are uncomfortable with ambiguity.** Review your approach to managing uncertainty and change, and include real-life examples and situations. Learn about their fears, help them determine their biggest areas of opportunity, and suggest your ideas for improvement. Coach them throughout an ambiguous problem and share your thinking and feedback regularly. Identify places in which they could have taken a better approach and how you've tackled similar problems in the past. Meet with them throughout the process to review their thoughts and concerns. Keep track of your activities and learnings in this area. Assess how effectively you coach and the outcome of progress made. Share your activities and learnings with your manager or a trusted advisor over time.

- **Host a virtual or live lunch-n-learn to discuss strategies for coping with ambiguity.** Prepare a discussion around what it means to manage change, maintain adaptability, and move forward without clear direction. Discuss common problems that people face when dealing with uncertainty, and help identify creative workarounds and solutions for overcoming them. Use past examples of successes and failures and encourage others to do the same. Share tips and advice, and recommend small action steps to help others practice and improve. Keep track of the work you do and the impact it seems to have on others. Share your activity and learnings with your manager or a mentor.

- **Develop a short presentation reviewing your strategies for dealing with ambiguous situations.** Include tips, best practices, resources, and real-world examples and cases to showcase your experience and knowledge. Include tips about maintaining composure and productivity despite uncertainty.

Host a virtual or in-person training session with people who want to improve in this area. As an alternative, share your presentation online: Shoot a short video and post it on YouTube, or create a PowerPoint presentation and post it on your own blog or on SlideShare. Keep track of your work in this area and share your learnings with your manager or a trusted peer.

- **Conduct one-on-one or small group training sessions about dealing with ambiguity.** Ideas include:

  - Maintaining composure, even when you must shift gears suddenly
  - Weighing pros and cons quickly
  - How to leverage your network for support
  - Helping others navigate through change

  Keep track of the work you do and the impact it seems to have on others. Share your activity and learnings with your manager or an advisor.

Behavior 4: Creates a Culture of Innovation

How comfortable are you with thinking outside the box? Leaders who create a culture of innovation use insightful, often unorthodox, methods to discover and develop new ideas, products, or processes that are viable to the organization. They demonstrate and encourage creativity within their team. They draw out innovative thinking from those around them. They are an advocate for innovation and consider failure as an opportunity to learn.

Ideas for improving this skill:

- **Push those around you to generate new ideas.** Over the next 90 days, take steps to build an environment in which creativity and innovation are appreciated and rewarded. Encourage your people to consider and deliver creative solutions, and reward them for trying new things. Try these techniques:

  - When a unique approach or solution is proposed, consider it carefully, and if possible, approve it. If an idea is not feasible, provide feedback on the pros and cons.

- ○ Host interactive brainstorming sessions and show favor for highly creative ideas, even if they cannot be pursued due to restrictions.

- ○ Finally, help those around you recognize the value in taking risks, even if it means failing. Pilot tests are a great way to mitigate risks by implementing ideas on a small scale. Talk about the value of "failing forward," or the importance of learning from failure, but being persistent.

Keep track of your work in this area, and share your learnings with your manager or an advisor.

- **Encourage out-of-the-box thinking within your team, while also teaching to work through resistance to change.** Truly innovative, wacky ideas often take others out of their comfort zone. Note when new ideas cause angst within your team, and openly acknowledge that innovation is sometimes uncomfortable. Show your own enthusiasm for and commitment to new ideas, while helping your people learn to deal with the ambiguity that often comes with them, by discussing the possible outcomes and fears during team meetings. Make a conscious effort to acknowledge new ideas and the fears they bring up during the next 3 months. Keep notes about how your attitude impacted others, and share your learnings with your manager or a trusted peer.

- **Learn how to lead with questions, rather than jumping in with "answers. "** Your role as leader includes empowering others to draw upon their own thinking and unique perspective in tackling challenges. Encourage open and thoughtful pondering of issues by asking questions. Dive deep using open-ended and "why" questions. Listen attentively to the answers; be willing to let go of automatically thinking, "I know the answer." Assess which types of questions and framing are most impactful as you interact with others. Over time, share your experiences and learnings with your manager or a peer. Identify and commit to using two or three ways you have discovered that help you lead with questions.

- **Initiate a "new possibilities" discussion group.** Once a week, set aside time with your team to explore new ideas and possibilities. Share inspired ideas with each other, read books and articles related to your industry and share what you are learning, or watch TED talks (www.ted.com) and conduct a post-video dialogue session. Explore the most interesting concepts shared and ask how others can apply these ideas on-the-job. Each week, create new discussion questions and be prepared to introduce new material. Rotate this responsibility and get everyone involved. Put this approach into action over the next 90 days. Share what you are learning with your manager or a mentor.

- **Identify any organizational barriers that may be blocking innovation.** These may include widespread fear of challenging the norm, lack of funding or other resources, or micromanagement (by you or others). Try this: Hold a meeting where you ask your team to list all the possible ways innovation is discouraged within your organization. Then ask them to propose solutions or alternatives that can be enforced within your own team, if not throughout the company. Show your commitment to their ideas by following through immediately and implementing their solutions. Share your team's work with your manager or a mentor, and ask for their support.

- **Celebrate wins publicly.**
  - *Recognize people who have suggested creative solutions that were successful.* During team meetings, take the time to point out successes (even small ones) and then ask the person or team to share what helped them be successful and what they learned from the experience. Put this approach into action for the next 60 days. Later, share your learnings and outcomes with your manager or a colleague.

- **Create forums and opportunities for your team to share best practices.** Host quarterly meetings where your people present challenges that they are facing. Ask other participants to weigh in on how they would handle similar situations. Brainstorm together to come up with creative alternatives. If possible, invite individuals from other functions to attend and participate. At the end of each meeting, wrap up by identifying which problems were addressed and what solutions were posed. Follow up to identify how the proposed solutions worked for each participant. Put this into action for the next two quarters. Later, share your learnings and outcomes with your manager or a trusted peer.

- **Read books that guide you in how to inspire innovation at work.** Suggestions include:
  - *The Progress Principle: Using Small Wins to Ignite Joy, Engagement, and Creativity at Work* by Teresa Amabile and Steven Kramer
  - *The Ten Faces of Innovation: IDEO's Strategies for Defeating the Devil's Advocate and Driving Creativity Throughout Your Organization* by Tom Kelley and Jonathan Littman
  - *Leading Innovation: How to Jump Start Your Organization's Growth Engine* by Jeff DeGraff and Shawn Quinn
  - *Power Questions: Build Relationships, Win New Business, and Influence Others* by Andrew Sobel and Jerold Panas

Dedicate at least 30 minutes per week to reading these resources. For a period of 60 days, make note of the things you learn and new things you'd like to try. Review these with your manager and a trusted peer. Discuss how you can incorporate these learnings into your routine.

Ideas for leveraging:

- **Conduct one-on-one or small training sessions to help other leaders encourage innovation.** Examples include:
  - Use effective brainstorming techniques.
  - Reward good ideas.
  - Turn "failures" into positive learning experiences.
  - Share best practices among team members.
  - Select topics that you feel passionate about. Encourage two-way communication. Make it relevant by asking the attendees for examples and questions.

Keep track of the work you do and the impact it has on others. Share your activity, learnings, and the impact you think you have on others with your manager or a trusted advisor.

- **Develop a short presentation about instilling innovation within workgroups.**

  Include tips, best practices, resources, and real-world examples and cases to showcase your experience and knowledge. Host a virtual or in-person training session with people who want to improve in this area. As an alternative, share your presentation online: Shoot a short video and post it on YouTube, or create a PowerPoint presentation and post it on your own blog or on SlideShare. Keep track of your work in this area and share your learnings with your manager or a peer.

- **Coach other leaders who need help nurturing creativity.**

  Help them determine their specific areas to improve, and discuss what hinders them from focusing on innovation. Share concrete suggestions for how to become a creativity advocate. If appropriate, have them observe you when brainstorming with your team. Meet with them regularly to review their progress. Keep track of your activities and learnings in this area and share them, over time, with your manager or a colleague.

- **Offer to lend your "advocacy for new ideas" skills to a project team.**

  Help a cross-functional team or a special task force responsible for driving important results. Offer to lead regular brainstorming or problem-solving sessions, and help it accept and work with any discomfort that comes from new ideas that arise. Keep track of the work you do and the impact it seems to have on others. Share your activity and learnings with your manager or a mentor.

Behavior 5: Motivates Others

We often need the cooperation and support of others to accomplish our goals. Motivating those around us is a critical leadership skill. Leaders who motivate others are persuasive and influential.

They leverage positive reinforcement to guide and inspire others and are committed to bringing out the best in their team. They lead by example and assert themselves without diminishing other leaders.

Ideas for improving this skill:

- **Practice sharing information to motivate your team.** As a leader, you have access to more information than your employees do. Share information that can help them do their jobs better. In addition, communicate more than just the facts. Take time to share "feel good" tidbits you've heard, in addition to project news and changes. For example, pass along compliments, exciting news about new products, awards your company has been given, and more. Keeping your people in the loop with this type of information will increase their commitment and motivation. Within the next 30 days, implement one of these ideas:

  - At the end of each day review your notes from your meetings and conversations, thinking about the people in your group who need to know the information. Write their names with a bold, red pen next to the notes to remind yourself to talk to them. After you have, cross out their name.

  - Begin each day with a group huddle, when you can quickly update everyone at once about company news, project updates, and such.

  Keep track of how (and how often) you share information, and note the effects this has on your people. Are they more responsive as a result? Do they show more initiative? Share the results with your manager or a trusted advisor.

  Discover what motivates your people. To coach your people effectively, you need to tap into what motivates them to change. Within the next 60 days, commit to analyzing the motivation of each of your team members. Ask them questions such as:

  - What excites you about your work?

  - What are your current challenges?

  - Are you willing to take risks to change? If no, why not?

In addition to asking them what motivates them, make your own observations. Notice which activities they spend their time on and what tasks seem to energize them. After you identify what motivates people, you can focus their development on areas and work that is important to them. Share your findings with your manager or a mentor.

- **Actively build trust to engage and inspire more effectively.** It will be difficult to motivate people if you don't already share a foundation of trust. Over the next 30-60 days, try one or more of these techniques to build trust:

  ○ *Share some personal information when appropriate.* Sharing information about your life outside of work can help others feel connected to you, especially if you are typically reserved or quiet.

  ○ *Admit to mistakes quickly to demonstrate accountability and humility.* When you make a mistake, quickly own up to it, apologize to those that were impacted negatively, publicly commit to fixing the issue, and develop a plan to keep the problem from arising in the future.

  ○ *Do what you say you will do when you say you'll do it.* Anytime you commit to doing something (big or small), put it on your calendar and push yourself to complete it before or by the due date.

  ○ *Invest in relationships and building rapport whenever possible.* Make time at the beginning of conversations to learn how others are doing. Ask questions such as, What did you do over the weekend? Is there anything new or exciting about you that I should know about? Ask people out to lunch or coffee and spend the time learning more about them outside of work.

Make note of which techniques you commit to trying and, for a period of 30 days, keep track of your efforts and learnings. Later, reflect on themes in results, what you found easy, and what you found challenging. Make note of your learnings and the outcomes. Later, share this information with your manager or a trusted peer.

- **Celebrate small successes.** Big achievements can be few and far between, so take the time to celebrate peoples' small wins. This can be as simple as writing a "great job" email, announcing the win in a team meeting, or hosting a happy hour at the end of a tough workweek. Put this approach into action for the next 90 days. At the end, reflect on how it has impacted your team's motivation. Later, share your learnings and outcomes with your manager or a mentor.

- **Show your commitment to your people's development.** Push yourself to take time and regularly observe your people in several work situations and scenarios. Ask to see key work products, observe key meetings, attend presentations, and be copied on important communications. Identify and record what your direct report does well and where they could improve. Share your findings formally (in one-on-one meetings) and informally (via in-the-moment feedback) as appropriate. Commit to implementing these new habits within the next 60 days. Keep track of what you do and what you learn. Observe if there are changes in your people's attitudes and commitment as a result of your attention. Share what you've learned with your manager or a trusted advisor.

- **Learn to communicate with passion.** During the next 60 days, observe leaders who sell their ideas and get people excited about the company. What do they do to communicate their passion? Then practice making presentations in front of a video camera. Watch your performance and compare it to the leaders you observed. Make note of the techniques you need to improve, including:

  - Speaking dynamically, with a high energy tone of voice, good volume, eye contact, and smiles

  - Demonstrating enthusiastic body language: hand movements, walking around with purpose, and nodding your head

  - Creating a compelling story

  - Presenting a clear call to action

Keep practicing in front of a video until your feel confident with your content and your delivery. Review your progress with your manager or a colleague.

- **Delegate important work to your people to show your confidence in them.** Delegating valued tasks to others can be a show of your confidence and trust in them, which is motivating. Over the next 30 days, take time to identify key tasks or responsibilities you can entrust—in whole or in part—to a direct report. Consider also opportunities you may have to authorize one of your people to do something as your representative (attend a meeting, deliver remarks, or email a senior leader). Depending on the scope of delegation, plan how you will transition the responsibility, in stages if appropriate. Having your direct report "shadow" you because you accomplish the task can be a great teaching and transitioning tool. The goal is to share or pass on accountability while simultaneously providing guidelines and autonomy so they can successfully execute. Evaluate the outcomes of having thoughtfully delegated important work, the morale or motivation level of those to whom you've delegated, and share your insights and learnings with your manager or a trusted advisor.

- **Show people that you value them during interactions.** Over the next 60 days, try one or more of these techniques to show others that you genuinely value them.

  - *Record, remember, and recall information about people.* When meeting people for the first time, repeat their name at least three times in the conversation to help ensure that you remember it. During your conversation ask them about something unique to them, such as where they grew up, who they cheered for in the Super Bowl, and so on. When you get back to your office, put the information you've gathered in your contacts. The next time you see them, recall the information from the last conversation and build on the conversation.

  - *Give people your full attention.* Commit to staying completely attuned when others are sharing information with you. Close your computer and put your smartphone down during these interactions. Look people in the eye, nod to show understanding, and try to reframe and repeat the messages you hear.

o *Ask people how they are doing.* Ask questions like: How's it going? Is everything all right? Look them in the eye, wait for their response, and then acknowledge it. Work on improving not only general questioning but also specific work project questions, such as "How are you feeling about the report results?" When possible, offer a suggestion and your assistance to help them. Record what you learn about each individual and how you responded.

Keep track of which techniques worked best for you in engaging and motivating others. Share your learnings with your manager or a mentor.

• **Encourage and host nonwork gatherings.** People are more motivated in their work if they have strong relationships with team members. Help facilitate some time for team members to get to know one another. Consider an informal happy hour or a team coffee break. Augment this by inviting team members out to lunch and coffee when possible. Use this time to get to know each individual and be sure to share information about yourself. Put this approach into action for the next 90 days. Afterward, reflect on how it impacts collaboration and commitment among your associates. Later, share your learnings and outcomes with your manager or a peer.

• **Read books that provide tips on how to optimize others' motivation.** Suggestions include:

o *Great Motivation Secrets of Great Leaders* by John Baldoni

o *The 8th Habit: From Effectiveness to Greatness* by Stephen R. Covey

o *The Best Place to Work: The Art and Science of Creating an Extraordinary Workplace* by Ron Friedman

o *Why Motivating People Doesn't Work...and What Does: The New Science of Leading, Energizing, and Engaging* by Susan Fowler

Dedicate at least 30 minutes a week to reading these resources. For a period of 60 days, make note of the things you learn and new things you would like to try. Review these with your manager and a trusted peer. Discuss how you can incorporate these learnings into your routine.

Ideas for leveraging:

- **Coach people who want to improve their ability to motivate others.** Offer to spend time observing them during team meetings and one-on-one interactions. Make note of what they could do better, and share your ideas and tips. Share personal stories of your own successes around motivating others. Encourage them to commit to making two or three changes to their approach based on your advice and feedback. Check in with them afterward to see how they're doing and give them feedback based on what you observe. Keep track of your activities and observations in this area, as well as feedback from the person you're coaching, and share them with your manager.

- **Host a virtual or live lunch-n-learn to discuss the importance of employee motivation.** Prepare a discussion around what motivates people, reward systems, and such. Use past examples of successes and failures and encourage the audience members to do the same. Share tips and advice and recommend small action steps to help others improve. Keep track of the work you do and the impact it seems to have on others. Share your activity and learnings with your manager.

- **Develop a short presentation teaching others how to improve their employee motivation skills.** Include tips, best practices, resources and real-world examples and cases to showcase your experience and knowledge. Host a virtual or in-person training session with people who want to improve in this area. As an alternative, share your presentation online: Shoot a short video and post it on YouTube, or create a PowerPoint presentation and post it on your own blog or on SlideShare. Keep track of your work in this area and share your learnings with your manager.

- **Conduct one-on-one or small group training sessions about different ways to motivate people.** Topics could include:
  - Celebrating successes
  - Communicating with enthusiasm
  - Aligning different motivation approaches for different types of people
  - Rewarding people for good work

  Keep track of the work you do and the impact it seems to have on others. Share your activity and learnings with your manager.

Behavior 6: Selects Talent

How comfortable are you with selecting talent? A leader who selects talent well is a good judge of talent. They ask relevant and probing questions during interviews. They accurately predict how individuals will perform in different situations and they assemble diverse, talented teams.

Ideas for improving this skill:

- **Define the criteria for open positions.** Before you begin searching for new talent, take time to create a thorough job description. Think hard about what you need currently, as well as what additional skills will help your team in the future. Ask yourself:
  - What will this position be responsible for?
  - Who will this position be interacting with most often?
  - What technical skills are essential for this position?
  - What interpersonal and team skills are necessary?
  - What specific experience do I need? Include number of years, type of industries, software expertise, and so on.
  - What should I be seeking that I don't already have on my team (skills, background, and more)?

Build a solid job description that includes your answers to these questions. Ask your HR representative for examples or assistance if necessary. A detailed job description is your #1 tool in ensuring you'll hire the right person with the skills you need. Put this plan into action over the next quarter, and note how it helps you locate more qualified and appropriate candidates. Share your learnings with your manager or a trusted advisor.

- **Improve your approach to interviewing.** Create a consistent process to drive consistency, efficiency, and effectiveness. Before each interview, set aside time to cull through all your available resources (job description, resume, and your priorities) to develop the most relevant questions. Create a structured outline for the interview that includes:
  - Introduction
  - Describing how the interview process will work
  - Asking questions about the candidate's work experience
  - Asking questions about the candidate's career goals
  - Asking questions about the candidate's fit for the role and the organization
  - Providing information about the position
  - Selling the company, when appropriate
  - Closing the interview by describing next steps

  Review your approach with a trusted peer and ask for feedback. When finalized, commit to using this structure for the next three to five interviews you conduct; note your learnings, including what worked and what needs to change. Review your findings with that same trusted peer or your manager.

- **Observe someone who is known for being an excellent interviewer.** Within the next 30 days, identify two individuals in your organization who are known for being strong interviewers. Ask each if you can observe them the next time they interview. Take notes during the discussion and, later, reflect on: How did the leader review the candidate's qualifications? How did the leader probe and challenge the candidate? How did they phrase their questions? How did they sell the company? What did they do that you found surprising? Debrief your observations with them to gain additional perspective. Note three to five specific techniques that you can incorporate into your own interviewing approach. Commit to doing so over the next 30 days and update your manager on what you learn.

- **Build a tough but effective interview question set.** Build a structured set of open-ended interviewing questions that you can use again and again with the jobs you most frequently fill. Focus on these areas:
  - Background/job history
  - Relevant experience
  - Career goals and aspirations
  - Decision-making and supervisory experience
  - Organizational fit

  Be sure to include questions that probe candidates to give you details about an actual experience, not what they "would do" but rather what they "have done." For example: "Tell me about a time when you experienced conflict and had to resolve it; you were faced with a challenging project under a tight timeline; and so on." Based on the candidate's response, continue to ask probing questions, such as "How did you go about doing that? What was your client's or manager's reaction?"

  After you complete your list of questions, review them with a trusted peer or Human Resources partner, and ask for feedback. Try out your interviewing guide and tweak as needed. Share what you've learned with your manager or a trusted advisor over the next 60 days. Share your interviewing guides with others tasked with interviewing candidates.

- **Search for talent in-house; don't assume you have to hire from the outside.** Some of the strongest talent can be grown in-house. Promoting from within is not only a great motivational tool for your people, but can also be of great benefit to hiring managers: Qualified internal candidates are usually more knowledgeable about the organization's goals and priorities, and have shown themselves to be great fits for the culture. Take time over the next 30 days to determine in which parts of your organization "bench" candidates for your positions may be currently working. Sometimes, this is obvious, but cast the net wide to include possible candidates from unexpected sources (different department, location, and such). After your potential sources are identified, commit to include talented candidates from those pools when you have a future or anticipated opening. Record your process steps and your insights. Evaluate what you have learned and what you might do differently on future hiring occasions to leverage internal talent. Share those action steps with your manager, Human Resource partner, or a mentor.

- **Polish your interview process so that candidates have a positive experience.** Remember that job interviews are a two-way process: You are deciding if the candidates are right for you, but the candidates are also judging whether you and your company are a good match for them. Ensure you're making the best impression by:

  o Showing good follow-through when setting up the interviews

  o Having someone greet candidates when they arrive

  o Clearly describing what they can expect during the interview process

  o Choosing the right people to participate in the interviews. You'll probably want one to two others to interview the candidate, in addition to yourself. Choose people who have different perspectives and approaches so that you can collect balanced feedback about candidates. Make sure you equip them with appropriate interview questions so that they are prepared.

  Put these guidelines into practice over the next quarter. Share your learnings and progress with your manager or a trusted peer.

- **Challenge your personal biases.** Consider if you have a tendency to hire people who think and act like you. Think about the last six people you've hired, or supported for hire, and make note of the following: Where were these individuals sourced? What similarities in backgrounds do they share? Did you like them? Which characteristics did you most value? Why? Now ask, What educational backgrounds would be completely different than the majority of these candidates? Business experiences? Race, gender, age? What value would there be in hiring people who are different than those you tend to select? Share your reflections with your manager and a trusted mentor. Ask them for their perspectives on the value of hiring diversity. Brainstorm ways to change your approach to finding and selecting talent, and track your progress over a 60-day period.

- **Make a team effort out of selection.** The next time you have an opening in your department, talk to your team about the requirements of the position and the approach you'll take to filling the job. Get their input regarding potential sources of candidates, and formulate a method of ensuring the best person for the position is selected. Include the team in an appropriate way; the team members may not have the final say in the hiring decision, but their input is valuable, so you might consider having the team take the final candidates to lunch or conduct a panel interview. Later, have a team debrief of the final candidates and ensure the conversation focuses on the skills, knowledge, and experience required to do the job. Afterward, make note of the steps you took and the outcomes. Share this information with your manager or a peer.

- **Get the most out of the team interview debrief.** Come to the debrief session with your own point of view about the candidates, yet with an open mind to hear the input of others. Share your hesitations and concerns about each candidate, and listen to those of other interviewers. Consider their viewpoints and perspectives. If you can't reach consensus about a hiring decision, consider if you should bring in the final candidates for a second round of interviews. Consult with your recruiting partner to determine the consequences if you do (or don't) choose to do so. Discuss the process with your manager or a mentor.

- **Read books that inspire innovative and creative talent selecting strategies.** Suggestions include:
  - *The Talent Management Handbook: Creating a Sustainable Competitive Advantage by Selecting, Developing, and Promoting the Best People* by Lance Berger and Dorothy Berger

- *Who: The A Method for Hiring* by Geoff Smart and Randy Street
- *Hiring for Attitude: A Revolutionary Approach to Recruiting and Selecting People with Both Tremendous Skills and Superb Attitude* by Mark Murphy

Dedicate at least 30 minutes a week to reading these resources. For a period of 30 days, make note of the things you learn and new things you would like to try. Review these with your manager and a trusted peer. Discuss how you can incorporate these learnings into your routine.

Ideas for leveraging:

- **Coach people who want to improve their talent selection skills.** Offer to spend time reviewing their approach to interviewing and selection. Determine what they do that is inefficient or ineffective. Guide them through the steps of making an effective selection decision. Encourage them to commit to making two or three changes to their approach. Check in with them afterward to see how they're doing. Give them feedback based on what you observe. Keep track of your activities and observations in this area (as well as feedback from the people you're coaching) and share them with your manager or a peer.

- **Participate in interviewing role-plays.** Pair up with those who need to improve their interviewing skills. Help them create a strong interviewing question set, and talk to them about the importance of listening and probing. Help them find the balance between over- and under-selling the company and the job. Then, play the role of a candidate and ask questions, allowing your partner to practice responding in a confident, informed way. Later, give her feedback about what she did well and how she can improve. Keep track of your activities and observations in this area, as well as feedback from the person you're coaching, and share with your manager or a trusted advisor.

- **Develop a tip sheet about best practices in selection.** Create a short document outlining tips for selecting external candidates for hire or internal employees for promotion. Consider using an outline like:

- ○ Understanding the requirements of the job
- ○ Incorporating those requirements into a question set
- ○ Conducting a challenging, professional yet effective interview
- ○ Probing to better understand the meaning behind responses
- ○ Answering questions from candidates about the job, company, and so on
- ○ Appropriately and effectively selling the job and the company
- ○ Working with others to debrief an interview

Keep track of the work you do in this area and assess the impact you believe it has on others. Make note of your learnings and observations and share them with your manager or a trusted colleague.

- • **Volunteer to be part of a selection team for a mission-critical job.** Creatively identify sources for qualified candidates, being sure to include a process for surfacing any internal candidates. Offer to participate on the interview team and create a question set that is relevant to the particular job. Assist with debriefing candidates after interviews have taken place, and help the team focus on the most important aspects of the job and skills and experiences of the candidates. Offer to team interview with those who may need or want help. Keep track of your activities and observations and, later, share them with your manager or a mentor.

Behavior 7: Develops Others

Think back to mentors and teachers you have had who had a profound influence on your growth and development. What approaches did they take and what qualities did they have? Leaders who develop others use a structured and sustainable approach to guiding, coaching, and developing others. They have a track record of developing great talent.

Ideas for improving this skill:

- • **When interviewing, assess candidates' propensity for development.** Hiring development-minded people will make development a priority within your team. Over the next 60 to

90 days, make personal development one of the criteria you attempt to uncover in candidate interviews—regardless of whether the person is interviewing for a managerial or individual contributor position. Ask behavioral questions that point to someone's interest and past experience with development. (For example, ask, Give me an example of a time you've developed a particular skill on your own. How have you helped others learn or develop a skill? What are the highlights of your current development plan? Given your career goals, what skills do you most need to develop? What is your plan for developing them?) Identify how prioritizing propensity for development impacts your selection decision. Make note of the work you do in this area and what outcomes result. Later, share this information and recommendations with your manager or a trusted advisor.

- **Delegate effectively.** Push yourself over the next 30 to 60 days to delegate—or "share"—challenging, skill-developing work whenever possible (for example, on project teams, with peers, with coordinators, or administrative assistants on your team, during special assignments, and so on.) Help others see the benefit of sharing work or "dividing and conquering." Offer yourself as a resource and work to see these shared or delegated tasks through to completion. At the close of the task or assignment, reflect on key learnings and offer constructive feedback based on observations. Keep track of your work in this area and share it, along with recommendations, with your manager or a mentor.

- **Identify new and different career paths.** Promotions are no longer the only way to move around organizations, and managers, with support from leadership, need to promote creative career paths to keep employees engaged and learning. Over the next 60 days, consider how your employees can gain new experiences. How can they learn from others? How can their interests and quality of life needs be linked to the needs of the business in a more flexible way? What currently inhibits people moving more freely around the organization, either on projects, part-time jobs, lateral moves, and so on? Record your findings and share this information with your manager. After incorporating the feedback, consider how to share this knowledge with your team.

- **Provide stretch assignments.** Experts agree that the most powerful development happens on the job. Therefore, make sure you give your people opportunities to learn and grow, such as:
  - Serving on cross-functional teams
  - Developing a new process for your group
  - Planning a team event or meeting
  - Taking on a new role within your team, such as meeting facilitator or administrative coordinator
  - Leading a new project, under your guidance

  These assignments should be in addition to, and complement, their regular responsibilities. Within the next 30 days, identify stretch assignments for your top performers, and review your plans with your manager or a trusted colleague.

- **Appreciate and leverage your high performers.** Within the next 60 days, analyze your high performers to identify the skills and behaviors associated with success. Make a conscious effort to recognize your high-performing team members for their skills and strengths; do this in front of others when possible. Do not assume your top performers know how much you appreciate them; tell and show them.

  Use the information you've gathered about their skills and behaviors to build "high performance" profiles that can be used to help your other people see what it looks like to be successful. Encourage high performers to become informal mentors by sharing their tips and expertise with others. Identify a specific talent or skill that they possess and ask them to formally present their tips, tools, and best practices with the rest of the group (virtual conference, blog, memo, and more). Attend the session and consider asking your manager or a mentor to attend as well to demonstrate your commitment. Keep track of your work in this area, and share your learnings with your manager or mentor.

- **Be in a position to notice and recognize your people.**
  Push yourself to take time and regularly observe your people
  in several work situations and scenarios. Ask to see key work
  products, observe key meetings, attend presentations, and be
  copied on important communications. Identify and record what
  everyone does well and where they could improve. Be specific
  and share your findings at your next one-on-one meeting and
  consider drafting a development plan together. Put this plan
  into action over the next 30 to 60 days and keep track of what
  you do, and what you learn. Keep your manager or a trusted
  advisor updated regarding your activities in these areas.

- **Engage in regular development conversations with your
  people and keep your commitments.** Ask each of your
  direct reports to schedule time with you on an on-going basis
  (for example, monthly or every 6 to 8 weeks) to discuss their
  development. Use this time to learn about their goals, reflect
  on their development plans, and share your observations about
  their potential. Keep track of what you discuss in each meeting and refer to it before the next conversation. At the end of
  the year, put your notes together and create a "year in review"
  to review progress over time, reflect on accomplishments and
  discuss the next steps. Keep track of your work in this area, and
  share your learnings with your manager or a trusted mentor.

- **Create opportunities for your people to interact with
  senior level people.** Over the next quarter, look for appropriate opportunities to invite your people to interact with senior
  people (meeting, lunch, presentation, or task force). If possible,
  task people to participate in some way (prepare an introduction,
  facilitate a small part of the conversation, or contribute to a presentation). Ask them to identify and record what they learned
  from the interaction. If they contribute something, give them
  feedback on their performance. Also, consider asking them
  for feedback on your performance as part of their observation.
  Keep track of your work in this area, and share your learnings
  with your manager or an advisor.

- **Inspire those you work with to develop themselves.** Recognize the importance the organization places on development by recognizing people who drive their own learning and self-improvement. Publically recognize those who leverage in-house training resources and tools as well as those who make progress on development plans. Highlight creative ways that employees learn new skills and expand their career. Put this plan into action over the next 30 to 60 days, keep track of your efforts, and share your learnings with your manager or a trusted peer.

- **Find a mentor who is adept at developing talent.** Within the next 30 days, select someone you admire and who has a track record of developing employees. Ask for clear, real-life examples of how she has helped people identify opportunities, grow and develop, and achieve career goals. Learn about her process, where she gets information, and how she makes decisions. Ask to sit in on development conversations and feedback meetings and record your observations. Ask her to sit in on your conversations and provide you with feedback. Take notes regarding her advice. Make notes of the themes and concepts that resonate the most with you, and keep a list of the things you plan on incorporating into your approach. Share your learnings regularly with this person or your manager.

- **Read books that inspire innovative and creative development of your talent.** Suggestions include:
  - *Make Talent Your Business: How Exceptional Managers Develop People While Getting Results* by Wendy Axelrod and Jeannie Coyle
  - *Bringing Out the Best in People* by Aubrey Daniels
  - *The Organizational Champion: How to Develop Passionate Change Agents at Every Level* by Mike Thompson
  - *First, Break All the Rules: What the World's Greatest Managers Do Differently* by Marcus Buckingham and Curt Coffman

  Dedicate at least 30 minutes a week to reading these resources. For a period of 60 days, make note of the things you learn and new things you would like to try. Review these with your manager and a trusted peer. Discuss how you can incorporate these learnings into your routine.

Ideas for leveraging:

- **Coach people who need to learn how to develop talent.** Help them determine their specific areas to improve, and discuss what hinders them from doing more in this area. Talk about best practices, tools, technology, and research to drive best-in-class talent development. Share concrete suggestions for how to get better in this area. If appropriate, have them observe you for a period of time during a talent development initiative. Meet with them regularly to review their progress. Keep track of your activities and observations in this area, as well as feedback from the people you're coaching, and share them with your manager or an advisor.

- **Conduct one-on-one or small group training sessions about different topics in talent development.** Agenda items should include:
  - Providing stretch assignments
  - Having difficult feedback conversations
  - Collecting and leveraging data from a 360° review or from gathering multiple points of view
  - Building and implementing high-impact development plans

  Be sure to make it relevant to the group by focusing on real-life challenges they're experiencing related to these areas. Keep track of the work you do and the impact it seems to have on others. Share your activity and learnings—and the impact you believe it has with others—with your manager or a trusted peer.

- **Host a virtual or live lunch-n-learn to discuss common challenges to developing talent.** Prepare a discussion about what it means to grow and develop people in a way that's linked to the business needs. Include topics such as modeling a learning mentality and delegating for development. Talk about ways that people who aren't managers and who don't have direct reports can drive learning and development nonetheless. Use past examples of successes and failures and encourage others to do the same. Share tips and advice and recommend small action steps to help others practice and improve. Keep track of the work you do and the impact it seems to have on others. Share your activity and learnings with your manager or a mentor.

- **Develop a short presentation reviewing your techniques for developing talent.** Document your best practices, including:
  - How and when to deliver feedback
  - How and when to create a development plan
  - The importance of regular development check-ins

  Host a virtual or in-person training session with people who want to improve in this area. As an alternative, share your presentation online: Shoot a short video and post it on YouTube, or create a PowerPoint presentation and post it on your own blog or on SlideShare. Keep track of your activities in this area—and the feedback from your attendees—and share it with your manager or a trusted advisor.

8 ———————————

Commit to a Plan of Action

Now that you've identified your greatest strengths and ways to leverage them, and your greatest opportunity areas and ways to practice and improve, you're ready to make some commitments. Documenting your plan and committing to specific actions and timeframes are the best ways to drive improvement in any area.

The purpose of this section is to help you create your own individual development plan that you can use over a long period of time as you continue learning, developing, and improving.

Individual Development Plan Example

Use the template in Figure 8.1 to create your own development plan. Refer to the list of best practices in the next section when creating your plan.

INDIVIDUAL DEVELOPMENT PLAN

The purpose of this Individual Development Plan is to help you build your skills. Use the book "Driving Career Results" as a reference when completing this.

This IDP Form will help you do five things:

1.   Look for themes in the feedback you've received in the past.
2.   Identify what you believe are your greatest strengths and your most important areas to improve.
3.   Discuss these with your manager and a trusted advisor. Update until you are aligned.
4.   Write specific action steps that will help you leverage your strengths and improve your opportunity areas.
5.   Track your progress and follow up with your manager or advisor.

IDENTIFY YOUR KEY STRENGTHS FROM AVAILABLE INPUT

1. Self Assessment from "Driving Career Results" Book

Key Strengths:

a.	
b.	
c.	

2. Past Performance Discussions or Feedback from Teachers / Advisors

Key Strengths:

a.	
b.	
c.	

3. Other Feedback You've Received

Key Strengths:

a.	
b.	
c.	

IDENTIFY YOUR AREAS TO IMPROVE

1. Self Assessment from "Driving Career Results" Book

Key Areas to Improve:

a.	
b.	
c.	

2. Past Performance Discussions or Feedback from Teachers / Advisors

Key Areas to Improve:

a.	
b.	
c.	

3. Other Feedback You've Received

Key Areas to Improve:

a.	
b.	
c.	

Figure 8.1 Individual Development Plan

Best Practices for Development Planning

Following are best practices that you should consider leveraging as you create and then work your plan over time:

- **Collaborate with others who have strengths in areas that you need to practice and improve.** Think creatively about who these people might be, such as former co-workers or students, previous managers or teachers, senior leaders within your organization, those in your community who work in other companies or industries, and so on. Ask them if they'd consider being a coach to you as you work to improve your skills in a particular area. Often, you'll find people appreciate being recognized as a potential mentor and are happy to help.

- **Commit to one or two simple, bite-sized development activities at a time.** Don't overcommit to yourself, which can cause you to be overwhelmed. Instead, start small, recognize your progress, and add more activities over time.

- **Make your goals measurable by assigning dates by which you'll complete certain activities.** You can even break these down into multiple goals by determining dates by which you'll find someone to collaborate with, when you'll meet with them, when you'll take your first actions, and such.

- **Keep track of your activities, progress, learnings, and outcomes.** The more you document, the more you'll be aware of your learnings and what leads to success. Taking notes in this way also helps you debrief and share your learnings with your manager, coach, or trusted advisor.

- **Ask for feedback.** Push people to be honest with you. Let them know before a project, presentation, or effort that, afterward, you'd like their honest feedback about how you did. Over time, you'll know who you can depend on to give you good coaching and input.

  Ask others you respect how they drive their own learning and development. You'll learn about new resources, organizations, and ways to build your **network**.

- **Evaluate your progress.** For example, keep track of activities completed, feedback received, collaboration partners, improvement made, work or school results achieved, and more. This can help you describe in concrete terms what you've done and, more important, what results you've achieved over time.

9

For HR Leaders Only: Tips for Implementing Self-Directed Employee Development

HR leaders are the champions of learning, development, engagement, and retention for their organizations. Not only are HR professionals in the ideal position to drive change and improved results in these areas, they are obligated to do so. The purpose of this section is to offer a step-by-step guide for HR leaders who seek to improve the way learning and development takes place in the organization.

This guide walks you through a number of recommended steps to successfully create an organization in which employees drive their own development. You may think there are many steps here, but this isn't simply a change for HR. All employees and people leaders in the organization are important and critical stakeholders, so change management is a fundamental consideration throughout this process. In addition, the steps outlined assume that HR leaders will build the business case for change, in addition to driving the implementation of the new process.

As you consider options for driving self-directed career management within your organization, check out Skillsify, Inc. (www.skillsify.com). This book is a companion piece to the SkillBuilder web-based application, which powers self-directed development for organizations. The content within the app can be customized to an organization's competency model, learning resources, branding, and so on. Or the app can be used with the exact same competency model and library of development suggestions that you find within this book. For more information, write: info@skillsify.com.

Identify the Need for Change

Identify the need for change. What problems exist with the current state? What results is the organization currently facing? These may include (in whole or in certain parts) unacceptable or increased attrition, low employee engagement, feedback from employees about the lack of learning and development opportunities, requests from managers for assistance in development planning, and so on. For more insights about the current state, talk with your peers within HR as well as senior leaders to identify the true problem and potential solutions. Document what you learn, including the problematic outcomes that are currently associated with the problem. Do your best to ensure that instituting a new process and set of tools—such as self-directed employee development—is the best approach.

Identify Key Stakeholders

In addition to HR professionals, who is most concerned about the lack of meaningful learning and development for employees? What business leaders are impacted by the current state and are passionate about changing the career management dynamics and outcomes within your organization? Talk to a variety of different senior business leaders about this issue, and what they think would solve the problem in a sustainable, measurable way. Be sure to represent leaders from different parts of the business and geographies. Get additional input from key people leaders (for example, those with large teams of employees working for, or under, them or those with critical roles reporting into them). Remember: Development is ultimately owned by employees and their managers and supported by HR. Therefore, it is important to engage business leaders in this process. Keep track of those with whom you talk as well as their opinions and recommendations. Later, this will be good input for building a business plan as well as identifying sponsors and supporters of your recommended change.

Gain Agreement on the Objective

Summarize the problem, recommendation, and desired outcome in a clear and succinct written statement. At this stage, don't get bogged down with graphic design, PowerPoint formats, logos, or messaging. Instead, focus on getting the content exactly right. Take this document to your key stakeholders and review it with them. Edit it with their input until you feel sure that you have the alignment needed to drive successful change. Ask others to provide feedback and push-back on your objective so you feel comfortable discussing and defending it to others. When complete, if the look and feel is critical, you can begin working on that.

Confirm Scope and Goals

Now it's time to determine what your plan will be. What is your future desired state? What outcomes will be important for which stakeholders? What results are you aiming for and who will be involved in ultimately getting there? What will the expectations and roles be for each stakeholder group involved, and how can efforts and outcomes be tracked? If possible, work with project managers who have experience leading such planning and implementation efforts. They can help you estimate key work activities, timeframes, decisions, investments, outcomes, and more. After you put your plan together, you can seek approval to move forward.

Get Approval to Move Forward

With your objective clearly outlined, and your high-level plan and estimates for timeframes, costs, and such completed, you can seek approval from the person who would be the *executive sponsor*. She may have additional questions and want information, and best practice research, so you might have to gather or complete this before you get the final approval to proceed. However, as with most big changes, the most essential work happens at the beginning, so stick with it if you believe self-directed career management can make an important impact on your business.

Develop or Identify Tools and Technology

When you are ready to move forward, identify the tools and technology you need to create a sustainable, technology-enabled, measurable approach to self-directed learning and development. Consider the companion app to this book: Skillsify's SkillBuilder tool (www. skillsify.com). It's a web-based tool that mirrors the elements presented in this book, including the self-assessment, click-to-build development planning, a huge library of development suggestions, and the capability to collaborate virtually with anyone. The tool also provides managers and HR leaders with access to dashboards and reports that track program activity and effectiveness.

Identify Pilot Participants

It's always recommended that you pilot a program like this to check your assumptions and to determine the best approach for achieving your desired outcomes. Because there are so many stakeholders involved in launching self-directed employee development (employees, hiring managers, senior leaders, HR professionals, and so on) it takes planning and testing to do it well. A pilot group may report to a senior business leader who is passionate about the topic of employee development, or it may be a group of employees who have been actively requesting more learning and development. Try not to pilot the new process with the best, most cooperative—or the unhappiest, disengaged—employee group because neither is likely to reflect the overall organization. Let the pilot group know that it has been chosen to test the process, that its patience and input will be critical, and that it will be asked for feedback about how the process worked and what can be improved in the future.

Develop Communications and Training Materials

A pilot should test your approach to a full rollout. Therefore, a suite of communications and training templates will be essential to your pilot. Begin by analyzing your stakeholders. Document every group who will be affected by this change. What are they currently doing versus what will they need to do in the future? What will close this gap from the current to future state, such as communication, training, accountability, and more? From here, you can create the tools needed to close the gaps for your pilot, including both communication messages and templates as well as training materials. The training materials for such a rollout may be simple, but it's still important to document and implement them thoughtfully. Ideally, during and after the pilot, you will get feedback from participants regarding the effectiveness of these materials and update them for future use.

Implement the Pilot

When all the tools, templates, and trainings have been developed and the technology you plan to use has been configured and tested, you can launch your pilot by training those who will be involved. Throughout the implementation of the pilot, get feedback from the group about what's working well, what should change, and what is missing. Use short, "pulse" surveys with pilot participants to assess, over time, how effective the changes are and whether the new process meets their needs. Get their opinion and input regarding aspects of the program such as the following:

- The Self Survey and results
- The Development Planning template
- The quality of the library of resources
- The ease of collaborating with others
- The interactions with managers

Depending on the feedback from the pilot, the training or the communication messaging or templates should be updated to address feedback and early concerns.

Track Adoption and Results

As the pilot proceeds, continue to gather feedback from the participants and as much relevant objective data as you can. This might include the number of plans created, activities being worked, number of participants collaborating with others, types of strengths and needs participants are choosing to work on, training and development resources they're leveraging, how many updates have employees had with their managers, and so on. As you gather this data, create a method for capturing and analyzing it over time. Also consider how best to assess the quality of the efforts in addition to the number of efforts. For example, you might survey managers to get their input on any behavioral changes they've observed among their employees who are testing the process. With all the essential data, you can determine the best way to review it with your key stakeholders, and what action you should take based on the findings and recommendations.

Expand More Broadly

If their results are positive, you'll want to gain buy-in and build the plan for expanding the pilot. An important part of this recommendation will be your findings and data-based outcomes from your pilot program. Not everything will have gone perfectly, so be sure to identify issues and opportunities as well as your plan for addressing them. You may not want to roll out the process everywhere quite yet, so determine the next steps and priorities for further implementations. Also have a succinct and meaningful plan for measuring further results and review it with your key stakeholders.

Conclusion

I hope you've found this book about self-directed learning and development meaningful and helpful. In our new economy, business and earning potential are powered by knowledge, information, and creativity. This makes it essential to drive your own learning, improvement, and career planning. You've already started down the path by reading this book. So, congratulations. Please let me know what you learn—and how we can improve in the future.

Linda Brenner
linda@skillsify.com

Index

organizational finance, 74-75
outlines (presentation), 129
overcoming obstacles
    definition of, 26
    improving, 99-104
    leveraging, 105-106
ownership, taking, 155-156
owning feedback, 151-152

P

passion in communication, 194-195
past experience, learning from, 35
people skills
    influencing others
        definition of, 24
        improving, 62-66
        leveraging, 66-67
    relationship building
        definition of, 24
        improving, 57-61
        leveraging, 61-62
    teamwork
        definition of, 24
        improving, 67-71
        leveraging, 71-72
performance plans, developing, 180
performance reviews, 1, 9
personal excellence
    accountability
        definition of, 28
        improving, 150-156
        leveraging, 157
    integrity
        definition of, 27-28
        improving, 145-149
        leveraging, 149-150
    intellectual curiosity
        definition of, 28
        improving, 158-161
        leveraging, 161-162
    self-development
        definition of, 28
        improving, 162-166
        leveraging, 166-167
personal values statements, 147

piloting new initiatives, 52-53
    expanding pilot, 220
    implementing pilot, 218-219
    pilot participants, identifying, 218
planning
    definition of, 25
    improving, 87-92
    leveraging, 92-93
plans
    development plans
        assessing improvement, 10
        building, 10
        collaborating with others on, 6-7
        compared to performance reviews, 9
        defined, 2-3
        encouraging employees to develop, 11
        evaluating, 6
        free training resources, 5
        functional versus soft skills, 7-8
        goal of, 4
        how often to write, 5
        HR role in, 9-10
        input from friends and relatives, 3-4
        manager's role in, 4
        promotions and, 8-9
        responsibility for creating, 3
        70-20-10 approach, 5-6
        topics included in, 4
    performance plans, 180
"post mortem" analysis, 46, 55
practicing presentation delivery, 133
presentation skills
    definition of, 26
    improving, 127-134
    leveraging, 134-135
prioritization
    definition of, 20-26
    improving, 93-98
    leveraging, 98-99
problem assessment, 32
problem solving
    definition of, 23
    improving, 31-42
    leveraging, 36